W9-CPM-254

Public Policy Skills

Third Edition

by

William D. Coplin

and

Michael K. O'Leary

Professors,
Maxwell School of Citizenship and Public Affairs,
Syracuse University

Copyright © 1998 by William D. Coplin and Michael K. O'Leary

All rights reserved

ISBN 0-936826-42-8

Printed in the United States of America

Published by:

Policy Studies Associates
P.O. Box 337
Croton-on-Hudson, NY 10520

Policy Studies Associates (PSA) was established in 1976 to develop policy analysis skills and to apply these skills to important public issues. An operating program of the Council on International and Public Affairs, PSA is a cooperative non-profit undertaking of a small group of faculty members, teachers, and other educators concerned with improving the quality of education on public policy issues in schools, colleges, and universities.

In 1986, PSA initiated the Effective Participation in Government Program to assist secondary schools, teachers, and students in introducing courses of study which emphasize informal participation in government and community affairs. EPG organizes teacher workshops, provides consultative assistance to schools, and publishes instructional material for teachers and students. For further information write: Policy Studies Associates, P.O. Box 337, Croton-on-Hudson, New York 10520; or call: 914-271-6500.

Acknowledgements

This third edition of *Public Policy Skills* has benefitted greatly from the reactions of more than 1,500 students at Syracuse University who have offered constructive criticism. Even more valued have been the comments of an extremely talented and dedicated set of high school teachers throughout New York State who have worked closely with us in Syracuse University's Project Advance Program. They have used the first edition in their classrooms and suggested many of the revisions that are included in this edition of the book.

We would also like to thank Kalpana Fernandez and Jessica White for the many hours they spent editing and revising the book according to the authors' notes.

The revisions of Chapter 2 on library research were drafted by Elaine Coppola and Pamela Thomas of Syracuse University's Bird Library. We appreciate their dedication to making our students better users of library information.

Finally, our thanks go to Judy Rizzi of Policy Studies Associates for the cover design and oversight of the manufacturing process.

About the Authors

William D. Coplin is Professor of Public Affairs, and Director of the Public Affairs Program of the Maxwell School at Syracuse University. As contributing author to the guidelines for the Regents twelfth grade required course (1988-89) "Participation in Government," Dr. Coplin was able to draw upon his years of teaching and expertise in public policy analysis and social science education. He has published more than 50 books and articles in the social science and political science fields.

Professor Coplin, who received his Ph.D. from American University, has received numerous teaching awards from Syracuse University including the Laura J. and L. Douglas Meredith Professorship for Teaching Excellence. He is a Director of Political Risk Services for the PRS Group plc, London, England and has co-authored with Michael O'Leary, *Power Persuasion: A Surefire System to Get Ahead in Business* (Addison-Wesley, 1985).

Michael K. O'Leary is a professor emeritus from the Maxwell School of Citizenship and Public Affairs at Syracuse University. In addition to his research and publications (totaling some 50 books and articles in the fields of international policy analysis, international economic policy, research methods, and teaching strategies), he is contributing author to New York State's guidelines for the "Participation in Government" course. Dr. O'Leary has also served as an editor of the monthly *Political Risk Letter*, and has provided political risk forecasting consultations to multinational firms in this country and abroad.

Dr. O'Leary received his Ph.D. degree from Princeton University. He taught there and at the University of Southern California and Dartmouth College before becoming a faculty member at the Maxwell School in 1965.

Table of Contents

Introduction

A public policy is a government action that affects what happens in society. Public policy decisions that affect your life are being made constantly. Where you go to school, what courses you study, which jobs are available to you when you leave school, when you are allowed to get a driver's license, and how fast you are allowed to drive -- are all results of public policy. To be part of--or at least understand--those decision-making processes in your local, state, national, and international communities, you need to acquire the skills necessary for analyzing and judging actual and proposed policies.

Public Policy Skills will help you to learn how to analyze public policy issues in a systematic and well-informed way. It provides you with the skills that are required to make intelligent judgments about existing and proposed public policies. Each chapter of this book is designed to help you complete some type of analysis. The first ten chapters present basic concepts of a problem-solving framework for the analysis of public policy. Exercises for these 10 chapters are available from a website described below. The remaining chapters provide the student with an introduction to intermediate level skills in the first ten chapters. Instructors may want to assign some of these chapters for additional required work or merely to advise students to refer to those chapters when appropriate.

Opening Sections

Each chapter begins with a goal statement that describes exactly what skills you will acquire after successfully completing the work in that chapter. A more general introduction follows which outlines how the chapter is presented and how the material covered affects participation in government.

Step Sections

Each chapter contains a series of sections called steps. Each step gives you a particular task, such as "Identifying Societal Problems," and then gives you the information necessary for completing that task. Sample applications are also included. The last step in each chapter is an application of that chapter's skills to the content of the news media. It is included to enhance your skills and does not need to be the same topic that you cover in the rest of the chapter.

Supplementary Materials on Website

Instructors can have students download the exercises and place them in a wordprocessing file so they can be completed as assignments to the book. The PAF 101 homepage can be found at http:\\www.maxwell.syr.edu/maxpages/classes.paf101/ index.html which is updated frequently and maintained under the Maxwell School of Citizenship and Public Affairs at Syracuse University. At this website you will find tips and other reccomendations on developing public policy skills.

Chapter 1

A Framework for Public Policy Analysis and Action

YOUR GOAL

To decide what you want to learn by identifying societal problems, public policies, and players.

Introduction

Public Policy Skills introduces you to the skills necessary to develop public policy strategies to make our society better. This chapter will help you to understand the educational purpose of this book and the components of public policy.

Deciding What You Want To Learn

This book will help you to achieve two different types of learning objectives:

1. Skills -- the ability to collect and organize information so that you can reach a decision about major public policy issues.

2. Understandings -- awareness of the causes and dynamics of problems in our society and what government can do about them.

Since you will be developing both your skills and your understandings throughout this course, it is important that you decide for yourself what you want to learn. To examine the skills presented, turn to the table of contents. From the topics covered, you can see the wide variety of strategies available to you for gathering information and working

1

to solve society's problems. The exact information which you acquire will be determined by the subjects to which you choose to apply your skills throughout the book. If you are interested in the problem of child abuse, for example, you might choose as your learning objectives such areas as the extent and causes of child abuse in a particular state; what, if anything, governments are doing to reduce the occurrence of child abuse in that state; and who are the key non-governmental and governmental officials interested in the problem.

Begin to think about what sort of skills and understandings you wish to gain. The rest of this chapter is devoted to introducing the basic features of public policy analysis.

Step 1.1: Identifying Societal Problems

A societal problem exists when something is "wrong" with some aspect of society. But how do you decide if something is wrong? By first deciding what you think the goals of a society should be, and then determining the degree to which societal conditions further these goals. Societal problems exist if societal conditions do not further these goals.

In carrying out your first step, deciding what the goals of society should be, you do not have to look very far. The goals can be found in the Declaration of Independence: "life, liberty and the pursuit of happiness." These are "unalienable rights" that Thomas Jefferson used in order to justify the American colonies' decision to break away from England. We will use this phrase as the guide to goals in identifying societal problems.

The terms "life," "liberty," and the "pursuit of happiness" need to be explained in more detail to provide a comprehensive guide to identifying societal problems.

Life: People want to enjoy good health and avoid the dangers of diseases, pollutants, and malnutrition. People would also like to enjoy personal safety unthreatened by foreign attack, street crime, unsafe roads, or dangerous products.

Liberty: People want to freely express themselves regarding politics, religion, and culture. They also want to be free to choose where they live, with whom they associate, and the style of life they lead.

Pursuit of happiness: This broad range of concerns can be grouped under two headings. First, economic opportunity should be open to all and should be in sufficient quantity to allow people to survive and enjoy themselves. Second, a clean physical environment is required for good health as well as personal satisfaction.

Figure 1.1: Six Societal Goals

Life	*Liberty*	*Pursuit of Happiness*
1. Good Health	3. Free expression	5. Economic opportunity
2. Personal Safety	4. Free choice	6. Clean environment

Making judgments about societal conditions relates to the six goals. A balance needs to be struck among the six goals because the extreme pursuit of one may reduce the amount achieved regarding another. For example, free expression that would allow someone to falsely yell "fire" in a crowded theater would reduce the personal safety of those in the theater.   A society dedicated to an excessively clean environment may find reduced freedom of choice because of strict regulation.

Whose Problem?

A **societal problem** is when some aspect of our society, or, as we will call it, "a societal condition," fails to meet one or more of the six goals. Of course, people interpret societal problems differently. For example, a societal problem for undergraduates at many universities and colleges is the number of closed courses. A closed class reduces the freedom of choice for the student and may even threaten the student's chances for economic opportunity. It is a pervasive problem that most directly affects undergraduates. Faculty, graduate students, and administrators may not see the number of closed courses as a serious problem. They may even argue that students avoid taking courses early in the morning or late in the afternoon which is why so many of the chosen courses are closed. The seriousness of the problem therefore depends on whose view is considered. However, if the number of closed classes leads to a situation in which undergraduates can not register for a full schedule or are forced to attend summer school, other groups may agree that it is in fact a societal problem.

For this reason, when you define a societal problem, you also need to discuss which groups are most affected by the problem and which of the six goals are being threatened. Some groups will always feel more intensely than others about the seriousness of a societal problem. In addition, groups look at the problems from the perspective of different goals. When you study societal problems, you need to be aware of these differences.

One final point: you must bring your own individual perspective to the application of the six goals. This book is not intended to make you an effective lobbyist for a specific group. One goal of this book is that you act to improve societal conditions generally. You should be aware of the legitimate preferences of others, but even more importantly you must decide which societal problems are most important from your own perspective as someone who accepts the goals outlined in the Declaration of Independence.

Where is the Problem?

The location or geographic scope of a societal problem also needs to be carefully considered. As Figure 1.2 shows, problems can exist in several places: local, state, national, and international. The problem can also be found within your local community, family, social group or organizations to which you belong.

Figure 1.2: Geographic Scope of Societal Problems

School Level
- Low student morale
- High absenteeism
- Poor academic
  performance
- Vandalism

Community Level
- High crime rate
- Deteriorating roads
- Population decline
- Too much commercial
  development

State Level
- Loss of business
- High levels of water pollution
- Increased traffic
  fatalities

National Level
- Escalating medical costs
- Decline in exports
- Federal budget
  deficit

International Level
- Famine in Africa
- High debt
- Acid rain
- AIDS epidemic

Analyzing a societal problem involves identifying the primary location of the problem. You will also eventually need to look at the interdependence between the primary location and other locations; what happens internationally and nationally frequently effects states and local communities.

Selecting a location or geographic scope will depend upon the availability of information as well as the purpose of your analysis. If you want to do something about the problem, you will probably need to work in a local community. If you want to obtain a broader view of the problem or you are completing a study for a course, you may want to study the state or national dimensions of the problem.

Step 1.2: Identifying Public Policy

A **public policy** is an actual or proposed government action intended to deal with a given societal problem. An example of a public policy is the New York State law which changed the drinking age from 19 to 21. There are three elements of government actions:

Legislation: The legislative aspect of public policy establishes guidelines to be followed by members of the society. A law raising the drinking age from 19 to 21 is intended to stop people between the ages

5

of 19 and 21 from consuming alcoholic beverages. Notice that a law does not necessarily mean that people will behave differently. Governments cannot make people do anything; they can only tell them what is legal behavior and punish them if they act illegally.

Administrative Acts: Administrative acts are what governments do to put a law into practice. They include such actions as: mailing social security checks; giving tickets to people who illegally park their cars; or scheduling when trash will be collected. Administrative acts are often even more important than the laws themselves. For example, if the police decide not to vigorously enforce the legal drinking age, the law will have little effect on those under 21.

Judicial Decisions: Judicial decisions take place when courts apply the law to a specific situation. They may have the effect of both administrative and legislative acts. For example, existing laws may be declared unconstitutional. The legal situation then returns to the situation that existed prior to the passage of the law. Furthermore, judges may issue sentences to law violators in ways that either increase or decrease the force of the law. For example, since the early 1980s, violators of drunk driving laws have received harsher penalties in part because of stricter judicial decisions.

All three types of government actions are required for any public policy. For example, to reduce the number of highway accidents, a state sets speed limits on its roads. Making and carrying out such policies involves legislation, administrative acts, and judicial decisions. The legislature of the state enacts general legislation; the Department of Transportation in the state determines the actual limit for a particular stretch of road; the police patrol the road and give tickets to speeders; and the local courts decide on penalties for violators of the law.

A second general distinction that is made when discussing public policies is the geographical location of government at which the action takes place. The four geographic locations of government actions are:

Local: village, town, city, or county
State: one of the 50 states
National: the entire United States
International: two or more national governments or
                     international organizations

6

You could conceivably consider hundreds of policies resulting from different government actions that are related to your societal problem. A complete analysis of all these policies is not possible. What you should do instead is identify the major policies already in place at different locations which address your problem before you start to analyze new policy alternatives. You should not reinvent an existing policy nor should you ignore policies that may be having the effect of reducing the problem.

Step 1.3: Identifying Players

Players are individuals, groups, or institutions that work to influence public policies. Players can be elected officials, appointed officials, organized groups, or private individuals who seek to shape policy.

Unorganized categories of people such as the public, voters, consumers, or taxpayers are not automatically players. To be players, these people have to take an active role in influencing players who actually have the authority to implement public policy. Do not assume people are players merely because they are affected by a public policy. Dog owners are affected by leash laws, but they are not players unless they organize to try to affect policy. To be a player, a person must be actively attempting to influence the public policy process. For example, some players involved in a law regarding a national speed limit are legislators, the President, the Department of Transportation, and the state police. A trucker's association which opposes the law, and the American Automobile Association (AAA) which supports the law, also qualify as players, since they are actively trying to influence public policy. Drivers are not automatically players because they are only affected by the law; they do not influence the players or necessarily work to influence the policy.

Step 1.4: Applying the Three Components of Public Policy Issues

You have now been introduced to the three essential components of a public policy issue.   Figure 1.3 below outlines how these three components interrelate.

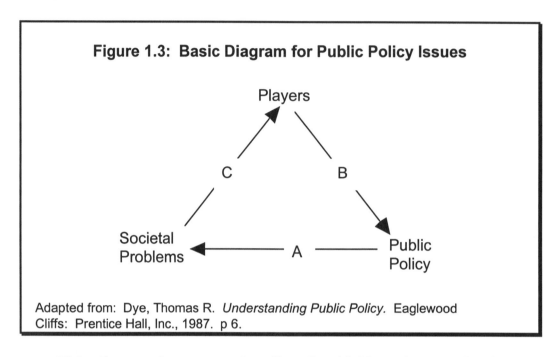

Figure 1.3: Basic Diagram for Public Policy Issues

Players

C   B

Societal Problems   A   Public Policy

Adapted from: Dye, Thomas R. *Understanding Public Policy.* Eaglewood Cliffs: Prentice Hall, Inc., 1987. p 6.

This diagram is a general outline for thinking about topics in this book. Societal problems motivate players to call for public policies that in turn affect the societal problem.   When analyzing any public policy issue, you should be able to identify the public policy, the societal problem, the players, and the relationship among the three components. Always ask yourself the three questions suggested by Arrows A, B, and C in Figure 1.3: (1) What is the expected impact of the public policy on the societal problem [*Arrow A*]? (2) Which players support and which players oppose the public policy [*Arrow B*]? and (3)   How does the societal problem stimulate the behavior of players [*Arrow C*]?

For example, here is how the three arrows from Figure 1.3 apply to a national speed limit.

Arrow A: The intended or actual impact of a public policy on the societal problems.   For example, the 55-mile speed limit reduces gasoline consumption and cuts down on traffic fatalities.

Arrow B: The position of a player on a public policy. For example, the AAA favors the 55-mile speed limit.

Arrow C: Societal problems motivate players to support or oppose this public policy. For example, a massive increase in the price of oil in the mid-1970s motivated Congress to implement the 55-mile speed limit.

Step 1.5: Selecting a Public Policy Topic to Study

Throughout the remainder of this book you will study one public policy topic in depth. You will be given a series of tasks in each chapter to enhance your skills of public policy analysis. To properly develop these skills, you will need to become as knowledgeable as possible about your topic. Although your instructor may allow you to switch topics, it will generally be easier for you to do a good job if you keep the same topic throughout. Keeping the same topic throughout will allow you to become an expert on the topic. Therefore, think carefully about what will interest you, what you are capable of understanding, and your capacity to acquire the necessary information. Here are some questions you should ask yourself to help make a good choice:

1. What societal problem am I deeply concerned about and why?

2. On what geographical setting (town, state, or country) should I focus in my study?

3. Do I have any background on the subject?

4. Do I know some people who are players, or have contacts with players whom I might contact?

5. Will I be able to apply Figure 1.3 to my choice? That is, am I sure that I have clearly defined a societal problem; do I have some idea of at least one of the major players; and can I think of at least one existing or proposed public policy?

Chapter 2

Using the Library
by Elaine Coppola & Pamela Thomas

YOUR GOAL

To learn how to use the library to gain information on your public policy issue.

Introduction

To use the library effectively, you need to know what information you need and how to locate it. Knowing what you need is something that requires a lot of thought as well as some preliminary investigation. Locating information, the main focus of this section, is a bit easier to do if you acquire some basic skills.

HINTS:

1. Information resources are now available in a variety of formats (e.g., print (paper), microform, and electronic). Sources are accessed in a variety of ways (e.g., on CD-ROM, through the library's catalog, through an Internet, or through a World Wide Web interface).

2. The title, content, coverage , and date of an information resource may differ from format to format. For example, the *ERIC* electronic database corresponds to two paper indexes: *Resources in Education (RIE) and Current Index to Journals in Education (CIJE).*

3. For the resources included in this chapter we generally give the most familar title and most commonly used format. Please check with your own library to find out what is available there.

4. The librarians and other library staff members are there to help you. Ask them for assistance if you are unclear about what

resources are best for your topic and for assistance in using those resources.

This chapter covers seven basic notes for carrying out research on many topics:

1.   Resource 2.1--Almanacs, handbooks, yearbooks, and other statistical sources

2.   Resource 2.2--Newspaper indexes

3.   Resource 2.3--Periodical indexes and abstracts

4.   Resource 2.4--Books

5.   Resource 2.5--United States government publications

6.   Resource 2.6--United States census data

7.   Resource 2.7--The World-Wide Web

Citations

Whenever words, ideas, or facts are taken from somewhere other than your own mind, they must be cited. There are specific forms in which sources should be cited. The style is different for just about every type of source, but, in general, citations should include:

> Author
> Title
> Title of Larger Work (if you are only using part)
> Volume Number
> Place of Publication
> Publishing Company
> Year of Publication
> Page Number

On the next page are examples of some of the different types of citations. Refer to: Gibaldi, Joseph. <u>MLA Handbook for Writers of Research Papers</u>. 4th ed. New York: The Modern Language Association of America, 1995 for the correct way to cite other sources including other electronic sources.

Examples of Citations

Book with an author
Roodman, David Malin. <u>Paying the Piper: Subsidies, Politics, and the Environment</u>. Washington: Worldwatch Institute, 1996.

More than one book by the same author
Frye, Northrop. <u>Anatomy of Criticism: Four Essays</u>. Princeton: Princeton UP, 1957.
---. <u>The Double Vision: Language and Meaning in Religion</u>. Toronto: U of Toronto P, 1991.

Yearbook
United Nations. <u>Statistical Yearbook, 1994</u>. New York: United Nations Publications, 1996.

Newspaper Article with an author
Dao, James. "Pataki Proposes Broad Reductions in State Spending.": <u>New York Times</u> 10 Mar. 1995, natl. ed.: A1+.

Newspaper article without an author
"Judge Rules Woman Who Provides Eggs Has Right to Decide Embryo's Fate." <u>New York Times</u> 17 Mar. 1995, natl. ed.: A12.

Newspaper editorial
"Death of a Writer." Editorial. <u>New York Times</u> 20 Apr. 1994, late ed.: A18.

Magazine Article with an author
Henkoff, Ronald. "Kids Are Killing, Dying, Bleeding.": <u>Fortune</u> 10 Aug. 1992: 32+.

Government Publication
United States. Bureau of the Census. <u>Statistical Abstract of the United States</u>. Washington: GPO, 1991.

World Wide Web Site
United States. Dept. of Education. "Standards: What are They?" <u>Improving America's Schools</u> (Spring 1996). Online. SyracuseUniversity.Internet. (June 16, 1997). Available:http://www.ed.gov/pubs/IASA/newsletters/standards/pt1/html

Resource 2.1:   Almanacs, Handbooks, Yearbooks, and Other Statistical Sources

Almanacs, handbooks, yearbooks, and other statisical sources give statistical and descriptive information in an easy to find format. These resources may range from the very general, encompassing most subject areas, to the very subject specific. Following is a brief annotated list of a few of the more widely used sources:

Almanacs

Information Please Almanac. New York: Simon, 1947-.

Contains a wide variety of information including extensive statistical information on the United States and other countries of the world.

The World Almanac and Book of Facts. New York: Newspaper Enterprise Assn., 1868-.

Includes statistics on society, industry, politics, business, religion, education, and other subjects.

Handbooks, Yearbooks, and Other Statististical Sources

United States. Bureau of the Census. Statistical Abstract of the United States. Washington: GPO, 1878-.

Provides a wide variety of statistics on the political, social, and economic situation in the United States. A good beginning source for all subject areas.

The Municipal Year Book. Washington: International City Manager's Association, 1934-.

Consists of articles, statistical data, and directory information relevant to urban affairs.

United States. Bureau of the Census. County and City Data Book. Washington: GPO, 1949-111.

Presents census figures for every county and for large cities in the United States as well as summary figures for states, geographical regions, urbanized areas, standard metropolitan areas, and unicorporated places.

County and City Extra. Lanham: Bernan Press, 1992-.

Updates, on an annual basis, the information found in County and City Data Book.

United States. Bureau of the Census. State and Metropolitan Area Data Book. Washington: GPO, 1979-.

Contains statistical data on a variety of subjects including health, education, employment, income, government, social welfare, and crime.

Digest of Education Statistics. Washington: GPO, 1975-.

Offers education statistics. Includes such information as the number of schools and colleges, enrollments, teachers, graduates, educational attainment, finances, and federal funds for education.

United States. Federal Bureau of Investigation. Uniform Crime Reports for United States. Washington: GPO, 1930-.

Provides statistics on all types of crime.

Resource 2.2: Newspaper Indexes

Newspapers are a valuable resource for obtaining general information on a topic. They are also one of the most readily available sources. The best way to locate newspaper articles on your topic is to use an indexing or abstracting service.   There are two basic types of indexes: those that cover a single newspaper, and those that cover more than one newspaper. The following is a partially annotated list of some newspaper indexes:

Newspaper Indexes Covering A Single Newspaper

New York Times Index. New York: New York Times, 1913-.

Christian Science Monitor Index. Boston: Christian Science Publishing Society, 1960-.

Wall Street Journal Index. New York: Dow Jones, 1958-.

Newspaper Indexes Covering Several Newspapers

<u>Newspaper Abstracts</u>. Ann Arbor: University Microfilms International.

Covers major regional, national, and international newspapers including: <u>Atlanta Constitution</u>, <u>Black Newspaper Collection</u>, <u>Boston Globe</u>, <u>Christian Science Monitor</u>, <u>Guardian and Guardian Weekly</u>, <u>USA Today</u>, <u>Wall Street Journal</u>, <u>Washington Times</u>.

<u>National Newspaper Index (InfoTrac)</u>. Foster City, CA: Information Access Co.

Indexes the <u>New York Times</u>, <u>Christian Science Monitor</u>, <u>Wall Street Journal</u>, <u>Washington Post</u>, and <u>Los Angeles Times</u>.

<u>NewsBank Index</u>. New Canaan: NewsBank.

Indexes only articles considered to be of research value from newspapers of over 450 U.S. cities. The complete text of the articles is available on the accompanying microfiche set.

<u>Ethnic Newswatch</u>. Stamford: SoftLine Information.

Covers articles from the ethnic and minority press in the United States including African American, Asian American, Native American, and Hispanic newspapers. It contains the complete text of the articles.

Resource 2.3: Periodical Indexes and Abstracts

For current public policy issues, valuable sources of information are found in magazines and journal articles, all of which are referred to as periodical literature.

Magazine and journal articles can be used to provide both background information and current developments in your public policy issue. In general, however, magazines tend to contain more general information; journals rely more heavily upon research.

Because many articles are published every year, you need some way to search systematically for those articles that are appropriate to your topic. This is done by using indexing and abstracting services. These sources list articles, most often by subject, and provide the article title, author, journal name, date, issue, volume, and page number.

There are two kinds of indexes:

1. General Indexes: These cover a large number of periodicals on a variety of subjects.

2. Subject Indexes: These cover a large number of periodicals on a particular subject such as education, social policy, or crime.

You normally can search indexes by subject and/or keyword, by author, or by title. Since it is likely that you will be conducting a search by subject, you will be faced with deciding which subject heading to use.

Start by thinking of several different terms to describe important aspects of your topic. For instance, if you were looking for articles on world hunger, you might come up with terms such as hunger, food supplies, famine, and drought. These could also lead you to related terms like desertification, rainfall, climate, and weather.   Once you have identified six to ten terms, look through the subject headings in the indexing or abstracting service to see if any of those words appear. If they do not, you will have to think of other terms used by the services that are relevant to your topic. Many indexes do provide cross-references to assist you.

For those indexes allowing keyword searching:

- do a keyword search first
- find a relevant article
- look at the subject headings used to describe that article
- then do a subject search using one of the relevant subject headings you found.

While there are indexes and abstracts covering every area of interest, certain indexes and abstracts will be more useful for public policy analysis. Many of them are listed below. Note that Readers' Guide to Periodical Literature is identified as a general index because it covers all areas, not just the social sciences. The others are focused more directly on the social sciences and, therefore, are relevant to a wide range of public policy issues. Also, the Readers' Guide indexes magazine articles, while the subject indexes and abstracts cover primarily journal articles. Below is an annotated list of some useful indexes:

General Indexes

Readers' Guide to Periodical Literature. New York: Wilson.

Covers popular, general interest magazines.

Periodical Abstracts. Ann Arbor, Mich.: University Microfilms, Inc.

Indexes academic journals as well as popular magazines.

General Periodicals Index (InfoTrac). Foster City, CA: Information Access Co.

Covers publicatons on business, management, social sciences, and humanities.

Subject Indexes

PAIS (Public Affairs Information Service) International. New York: PAIS.

Indexes current literature on economic, social, and political conditions. Includes books, government documents, and journal articles. Useful for researching all areas of public policy.

Sociofile. Norwood: SilverPlatter.

Covers sociology and related disciplines. Excellent for social policy issues. It corresponds to two paper indexes: Sociological Abstracts and Social Planning/Policy & Development Abstracts (SOPODA).

ABI/Inform Ann Arbor: UMI

Covers articles in business and management journals.

Black Studies. New York: G.K. Hall.

Indexes materials by and about African Americans, Africa, and peoples of African ancestry.

Business Periodicals Index. New York: Wilson.

Indexes, by subject, articles in English-language periodicals on business, management, and related topics.

Criminal Justice Abstracts. Monsey: Will Tree.

Contains abstracts of the current books, journal articles, and reports in the field of crime and criminal justice.

Social Sciences Index. New York: Wilson, 1974-.

Indexes more than 200 periodicals in the various fields of the social sciences: anthropology, area studies, economics, environmental science, geography, law and criminology, medical sciences, political science, psychology, public administration, and sociology.

Social Sciences Citation Index. Philadelphia: Institute for Scientific Information, 1973-.

International interdisciplinary index to social science literature.

ERIC. Norwood: SilverPlatter.

Covers research reports and articles in the field of education. It corresponds to two paper indexes: Resources in Education (RIE) and Current Index to Journals in Education (CIJE).

HAPI, Hispanic American Perodicals Index. Los Angeles: UCLA Latin American Center Publications.

Covers articles on a broad range of subjects to U.S.-Hispanic and Latin American topics.

Human Resources Abstracts. Beverly Hills: Sage.

Covers material related to social and labor problems.

Social Sciences Citation Index. Philadelphia: Institute for Scientific Information.

Provides an international interdisciplinary index to the literature of the social sciences.

Social Sciences Index. New York: Wilson.

Indexes periodicals in the various fields of the social sciences: anthropology, area studies, economics, environmental science, geography, law and criminology, medical sciences, political science, pyschology, public administration, and sociology.

<u>Women's Resources International</u>. Baltimore, MD: National Information
Services Corp.

Contains abstracts from a wide range of periodicals dealing with topics concerning
women.

Resource 2.4: Books

Although much of the information required for research can be found
in journals and newspapers, you often need in-depth, detailed information
which can only be found in books. By becoming familiar with the system
of organization in your library, the job of locating books becomes much
easier. Books are found on shelves by their call number.

Most libraries use one of two major coding systems for organizing a
library collection: the Library of Congress System or the Dewey Decimal
System. Under both these systems, the call numbers separate materials
by subjects. A different call number is assigned to each item in the library.
Under the library of Congress System, the books are coded by a
combination of letters and numbers, beginning with a letter or letters. The
Dewey Decimal System uses 10 major categories each beginning with a
number. Your library's catalog will give you the call number of the item
you wish to locate.

The best place to begin to find materials on a particular topic is to do
a subject search or a keyword search.

Usually a subject search means that you choose words from a
controlled (i.e., established) vocabulary. In colleges and universities
throughout the United States, the controlled vocabulary often used is the
Library of Congress Subject Headings.

A keyword search means you use whatever words you think describe
your topic. You can then review the citations retrieved, look at the subject
headings used in records most relevant to your topic, and refine your
searching by doing specific subject searches.

Resource 2.5: United States Government Publications

Every year the United States government publishes hundreds of thousands of pages of material on thousands of different subjects. These materials can be very valuable in studying public policy issues. Remember that these materials may be available in print (paper), microfiche, or electronic format.

U.S. government publications can be located in two basic ways:

1. Check your library's catalog. Many libraries include their government publications in their catalog.

OR

2. Consult the Monthly Catalog of United States Government Publications. To use the Monthly Catalog:

- Check the subject index for terms relevant to your public policy issue. There is a title index if you already know the title of the publication you are looking for. You can also consult the author index if you know the name of the government agency associated with the topic.

- Record the entry number which you then use to locate the full entry or bibliographic citation. Among other details, each entry gives the entry number, the author (person or agency), the title, the date, and the Superintendent of Documents (SuDoc) Number.

- Locate your document. These may be arranged in two ways: either cataloged and shelved in the general library collection along with other books, or arranged according to SuDoc number and shelved in the government publications collection. Consult the librarian on how the collection is organized.

In addition, the American Statistics Index (ASI) is a particularly useful source. It assists in finding statistics that appear in the thousands of government publications published annually. The ASI is published in two parts for each year: Index and Abstracts. The Index provides information by subject, author (which may be individuals or agencies), and category. The Abstracts provide bibliographical data, descriptions of the subject matter, and outlines of content with references to specific page ranges.

Here are four steps to follow in using ASI:

- Search the Index to identify publications of interest.

- Note the accession numbers.

- Use the accession numbers to locate and review the abstracts in the ASI Abstracts volume for information on the contents of publications. The most current year will be in paper form as an unbound supplement.

- Obtain the publication for complete reference.

Please Note: Both the Monthly Catalog and the American Statistics Index are available in both paper and electronic formats. Consult with your librarian to see what is available.

Should more information on government documents be needed, read:

Morehead, Joe. Introduction to the United States Public Informaton Sources. 5th ed. Englewood, CO: Libraries Unlimited, 1996.

Please Note: Local, state, and international government documents are also excellent sources of information. Consult your librarian for information about documents in your library.

Resource 2.6: United States Census Data

Special types of government documents are published by the United States Bureau of the Census. Every ten years the Bureau collects information on population and housing for the entire country. This information is updated within the ten-year period through estimates and sample surveys.

The Census Bureau breaks down the nation in several ways (for 1990 data):

1. **Regional/Division:** There are four census regions (west, south, northeast, and north central) each composed of two or more

divisions. Divisions are areas composed of groupings of contiguous states.

2. **Metropolitan Statistical Areas (MSAs):** A MSA is comprised of one or more counties containing a central city of 50,000 or more. All counties in MSAs are termed "metropolitan," and all others "non-metropolitan."

3. **Urbanized Areas (UAs):** A UA contains a central city plus the surrounding, closely-settled urban fringe or suburb, with a population of 50,000 or more.

4. **Urban/Rural:** The urban population comprises all persons living in urbanized areas and in places of 2,500 or more outside urbanized areas. Everyone else is considered rural.

5. **Census Tracts/Block Numbering Areas (BNAs):** Subdivisions of counties averaging 4,000 inhabitants. Tracts are defined by local communities and are frequently used to approximate neighborhoods.

6. **Block Groups (BGs):** Subdivisions of tracts and BNAs. A BG is comprised of all blocks with the same first digit in any given census tract or BNA.

7. **Blocks:** Blocks are areas generally bound by streets, other visible features, and the boundaries of governmental units.

The Census Bureau gathers information on many items under the two main headings of population and housing. Information gathered from all inhabitants (the 100% survey) includes:

Population Items
- Relationship to head of household
- Age
- Sex
- Hispanic Origin
- Race
- Marital Status

Housing Items
- Number of housing units at this address
- Owner/Renter

- Vacancy characteristics
- Persons in group quarters
- Rooms per unit
- Value

More detailed information is gathered from a smaller percentage of the population (the sample survey) and includes additional population items (e.g., education, language spoken at home, and occupation) and housing items (e.g., number of bedrooms, plumbing and kitchen facilities, and heating fuel).

The information gathered is compiled in a series of reports covering a variety of areas and subjects. To find a specific subject from the 1990 Census, the best source is the 1990 Census of Population and Housing. A general guide to the use of census data is the Census Catalog and Guide 1991. Some Census material can also be accessed through the Bureau's Web site: http://www.census.gov/

Resource 2.7: The World-Wide Web

The World-Wide Web is a part of the internet that is experiencing rapid growth and continual change. Because government information is usually copyright-free, you can find quite a bit of valuable information on the Web. Many educational and commercial organizations as well as individuals also post information on the Web.

The Web contains much useful information, but also contains much that is out-of-date, biased, or just plain wrong. You must carefully evaluate Web sources for relevancy, bias, accuracy, and completeness. In general confine your sources to those provided by governments, well-known news organizations, and authentic educational organizations. And, remember that even these sources may contain propaganda and self-serving information.

You may wish to start your search with one of the following sites. Remember that Web addresses and contents are subject to change.

Federal Web Locator: helps locate web sites of U.S. federal departments and agencies:
      http://www.law.vill,edu/fed-agency/fedwebloc.html

Government Printing Office Access: Includes Congressional bills, calendars, Directory, documents, Record, Record indexes, Reports, Federal budget, Economic Indicators, Federal Register, Government Printing Office reports, Government Manual, history of bills, public laws, etc.:

      http://www.access.gpo.gov/su_docs/

Thomas: U.S. Congress; good for legislative information (e.g., bills, and the Congressional Record):

      http://thomas.loc.gov/

Chapter 3

Using Surveys

YOUR GOAL

To define the purpose, select the sample, write the questions, plan the method of contact, and estimate the costs for a survey.

Introduction

Surveys can be a vital source of information for the study of current public policy issues. They range in form from open-ended, free-ranging interviews of a few key public officials, to a mail survey of thousands of people. They can provide unique information not available from other sources. This chapter introduces you to the basic principles of survey design.

Step 3.1: Determine What Your Client Wants

Surveys are a means for gathering information about societal problems, about players, and about policies. When you plan a survey, consider first who will be using the information you gather and for what purpose they want the information. You might conduct a survey for a government official who wants to assess the impact of a policy, for a non-profit agency that seeks more information on its clients, or for a pressure group hoping to use the results to support its views. By considering for whom the information is to be gathered and for what purpose they hope to use it, you will have a clearer picture of what questions to ask and what people you will need to approach for answers. For example, an Assistant Superintendent of Schools may want a survey conducted on students who drop out of high school in the local school district. Others in addition to your client, such as the school board, the parent-teacher organization, students, and other players might also use the data you collect.

Although your purpose is to gather accurate information for your client, the way questions are posed, as well as other research decisions, may introduce biases. The key test is the degree to which the procedures used to collect the information are a reasonable approach to acquiring accurate information.

Conduct surveys only for clients willing to allow you to follow proper procedures. The proper purpose of a survey is not to prove a point, but to gather and report information that will help players make good decisions. For example, a survey should not be conducted to prove that all people feel the seat belt law deprives them of their liberty; rather, a survey could be conducted to discover what people are saying about their unwillingness to obey the seat belt law in order to see if new laws are needed. A survey never tells you whether a policy is good or bad, or whether it should or should not be implemented. It only gives you information on conditions, people's attitudes, people's behavior, or their perceptions of facts that players can use as one factor in deciding how to deal with societal problems.

You may obtain factual and attitudinal information with surveys. **Factual information** consists of such things as the occupations of a particular group of people, their incomes, their reported behavior, their physical environment, or their use of various government services. For example, a study of mandatory seat belt use in New York State might ask people whether or not they personally use seat belts. The information derived from such a question would indicate how many people say they use seat belts.

Attitudinal information indicates how people feel and think about societal problems or about public policies designed to deal with those problems. In the mandatory seat belt example, a survey might determine if people feel more secure when they wear seat belts. In order to design and implement a useful survey, determine whether you are seeking attitudinal or factual responses for each question you design.

The preceding discussion will help orient you to completing successfully the steps listed at the beginning of this section. Pay close attention to the fit between the client's goals and the information your survey will provide. The best first step is to ask what the client wants to find out and then to make sure that it is compatible with the client's goals.

Sometimes, you may need to ask the client to more clearly state the goals and then to check to see if the questions are compatible.

A key element in determining the client's purpose is to clearly identify the target population. The **target population** is the entire group of individuals about whom you want to gather information. Make sure that your client agrees about the group of people whose views are sought. Without this, the client's purpose is unclear and the survey will be useless.

A target population must be carefully defined in ways that are appropriate to the particular questions you are examining. The most well-known types of surveys are public opinion polls of the entire adult population such as a survey to find out the preferences of the public for candidates in an upcoming election. However, smaller sample surveys of specialized target populations are usually more valuable for policy analysis because key groups of people may be more knowledgeable about policy, are more directly affected by a particular policy, or are in a better position to influence policy. For example, in a survey of the uses of food stamps, a sample drawn from the users of food stamps would be more appropriate than a sample drawn from the general population.

Defining a target population appropriate to your purpose involves determining its approximate size and geographical scope. For example, your target population could be the 12,000 doctors who work in a local community. Unless you are specific about the size and location as well as who is included, you cannot design a useful survey. When defining the target population, make sure that the reader of your final report will be able to determine who is and who is not in the target population.

Step 3.2: Choosing a Sample Population

The sample consists of those individuals chosen from the total target population from which you gather information. In seeking a sample, you have to make decisions about two questions, "How big should the sample be?" and "What procedures should be used to select the individuals in the sample?" Since in most cases, it is impossible to survey everyone in the target population, you will want to generalize the responses obtained from your sample to the entire target population. Therefore you must attempt to select as your sample a group of individuals that is representative of the target population. The goal of

27

sampling is to select a group of subjects whose responses would be a little different than if everyone in the target population responded to the survey.

The term **sample size** refers to the actual number of responses to your survey you receive, not the total number of individuals that you contact from some list or other source of potential respondents, called the sampling frame (O'Sullivan & Russel 114). As we shall discuss below, in some procedures, the response rate may be very low, requiring you to contact a large number of potential respondents in order to obtain a sample of adequate size. This section gives you some general guidelines on determining what your sample size should be.

The size of a sample is primarily determined by the resources you have available, the kind of analysis you will be undertaking, and the desired accuracy. To a much smaller degree, the size of the target population should also be taken into account. In general, the larger the sample, the better. However, obtaining a large sample is very costly in terms of time and money, so carefully calculate how large a sample you will need. Work to obtain a sample of the requisite size, but do not gather a sample larger than you can afford.

In deciding on sample size, consider what analysis of subgroups of the sample you will be carrying out. In a study of the use of food stamps in a particular county, for example, your sample of food stamp users might be analyzed according to the distribution of such important features as age, gender, and income level. The characteristics of the population may be extremely important in some cases. For example, surveys may show differences between females and males on questions pertaining to abortion rights and similar topics. Racial and ethnic differences tend to be strongly associated with opinions on racial equality.

These considerations should shape your decision on the size of the sample. For example, you may obtain a sample of 500, which is an adequate sample for most purposes. But you may be interested in comparing different subgroups of that sample, such as categories defined by age, occupation, sex, or other important features. In such a situation, you will wind up analyzing subgroups much smaller than the total of 500 and the confidence interval will be accordingly much wider. If you identify five occupational groups, for example, each such group might average only 100, and some groups may be much smaller if the sample is not equally distributed among the occupational groups. The more subgroups that you want to analyze, the bigger the sample should be.

The most important aspect of a sample is its absolute size: 100, 500, 1,000, or whatever. The number in the sample is much more important than what proportion of the total population this number represents. This principle of sample selection is sometimes difficult to grasp by novice survey researchers. Nevertheless, the fact that a sample consists of 500 individuals, for example, is more important than whether the number 500 represents .1%, 1%, 10%, or some other percentage of the target population. (This assumes that the sample was randomly selected.) Accurate samples of the total United States population can consist of fewer than 1,500 people. A sample of this size represents only about .00001 of the total population, but when correctly selected, can usually give an accurate representation of the entire population.

The size of the sample is most important because it determines what is called the *confidence interval*. The idea behind a confidence interval is that it gives you an estimate of how close the findings generated by the sample would be to the findings if everyone in the target population were surveyed. The confidence interval procedure can be used only with samples that are selected randomly. (See the next section on sample selection.) The confidence interval tells you the likely difference between the results of your sample and the actual situation in the entire target population.

In general, the larger the absolute size of the sample, the smaller the range above or below a reported number the confidence interval will be. For example, if you obtained an approval rating of 58% from a sample of 100 respondents, the confidence interval would be +10%. In other words, in 95% of the cases of a hypothetical repeated survey sampling, the approval rating would be in the range of 48%-68% (58% + 10%). If you obtained the same 58% from a sample of 350, the 95% confidence interval would be +5%, or 53%-63%, a much smaller range within which you could be confident that the results would fall 95% of the time.

Figure 1 displays the minimum 95% confidence interval for a given sample size, that is the confidence interval when the random sample is a small percentage of the target population. When a sample represents nearly all the target population, its 95% confidence interval number is smaller. Books covering survey research contain more complex tables that provide confidence intervals for graphs that represent a large percentage of a population. Figure 1 is a conservative estimate useful for most purposes.

Figure 1: 95% Confidence Interval (For Simple Random Samples Only)

Sample Size	There is a 95% chance that the figure in the target population will be within the following percentage (either plus or minus) of the figure in the sample.
30	18%
35	17%
40	15%
50	14%
60	13%
70	12%
80	11%
90	10%
100	10%
120	9%
140	8%
160	8%
180	7%
200	7%
250	6%
300	6%
350	5%
400	5%
600	4%
700	4%
800	3%
900	3%
1000	3%
1500	3%
2500	2%

Source: Calculated from Elizabethann, O' Sullivan and Gary R. Russell, Research Methods for Public Administrators White Plains, NY, Longmans: 1994, p. 147.

Using this table, you can choose your sample size by deciding how big the range of your results you are willing to accept. A sample of over 1,500 will give you the small range of +3% while a sample of 100 will give you a range of +10%. If you are unable to obtain a sample that is large enough to give you a small range, you should still report the findings to your client and recommend to your client that a larger sample should be taken. Most people find confidence intervals above ± 5% to limit the scope of the findings substantially.

Sample Selection

Samples can be selected using either *random* or *non-random* methods. In survey research, the word random refers to a specific procedure in which all subjects have an equal chance of being selected. In this case, random does not mean haphazard or arbitrary as it frequently does in ordinary conversation.

By contrast, in **non-random sampling**, subjects are not selected by chance. Non-random sampling is also called **convenience sampling**. Examples include contacting shoppers at a shopping center, or calling up the first 100 people on a phone list. Surveys based on non-random sampling cannot be generalized reliably beyond the people actually surveyed.

A sampling procedure must be evaluated by its ability to satisfy the objectives of the survey, given the amount of time and money available. Although random sampling is preferred in every case, time and respondent availability sometimes make it very difficult. Two of the most frequently used random sampling methods are called **simple random sampling** and **cluster sampling**.

In order to employ simple random sampling, you need access to a complete list of everyone in a target population and you must have equal access to all members of the population. Using such a list, you can begin at a randomly selected point, and select a sample from the list, skipping enough names as you proceed through the list to pick the names you will attempt to contact. For example, you may start with the 6th name on the list and choose every 20th name thereafter. A more widely accepted procedure among professional survey researchers is to use a random number table, which is a list of numbers generated by a computer that has no pattern.

If you are planning to select a sample from a target population of a particular group, you will probably be able to obtain a membership list from which you can randomly select respondents. Telephone numbers and addresses are usually available from such lists, but be aware that the lists may contain inaccuracies. The older the list and the less organized the group, the more inaccurate the list. In some cases, a client may want you to generate a target population from several lists. For example, a social service agency may ask you to obtain the membership lists of all churches in a specific area. The combination of these lists would then constitute the target population, although each list may vary in quality.

If you are planning to draw a sample from the general population, no comprehensive list of all members exists. A telephone directory comes close to such a list, since about 90% of all homes contain telephones. However, those people who lack telephones, such as the low-income, the elderly, and rural residents, may introduce biases in a sample that is drawn from the telephone directory. In addition, many people maintain unlisted telephone numbers or have two or more numbers. Depending on the purposes of your survey, such under-representation may or may not represent a problem. If it is a problem, a variety of techniques can be used to compensate for such sampling problems, as discussed below.

An alternative source listing of households for many medium-sized cities is a series of publications called the *Polk Directories*, published by R.L. Polk and Company of New York, which may be available in your local library. These directories list the names, telephone numbers, and addresses of city residents, so they can be used for face-to-face, telephone, or mail contacts. There are also CD-ROMS of phone numbers available that can be used.

In the absence (or unavailability) of a complete list of everyone in your target population, you cannot employ simple random sampling, but you can still use a method that is almost as good, and is widely used by professional survey researchers. This is the procedure called *cluster sampling*.

To use cluster sampling, first identify a series of locations where your target population may be found (such as classrooms, residence halls, or areas of a city). Obtain (or create) a complete list of such locations, and randomly select locations from this list. At each location selected, contact enough individuals to fulfill your goals for a sample.

These procedures are used in choosing national samples of the American population: randomly selecting states, counties, and regions within counties. It can be used in any situation in which you can develop a method for selecting individuals from a randomly chosen location.

Sampling Bias

No matter what sampling procedure you use, be sensitive about over-sampling or under-sampling certain categories of respondents, unless you have some reason for over-sampling certain key subgroups. For example, a list of all the doctors in a certain region may not be completely up to date and thus will underreport younger doctors and those who have recently moved into the area. As previously mentioned, sampling from the telephone book will result in some bias. It will bypass any individuals who do not own a telephone or who have some unlisted telephone numbers.

To check for sampling bias, compare key characteristics of the respondents in your sample to those in your target population. Your goal is to achieve the same percentages in your sample as in your target population. A perfect match is almost never achieved. But, at minimum, you should report how close or divergent your sample and target populations are with respect to key characteristics. Beyond this, you can report the significance of any difference, and take some actions to reduce problems caused by any significant differences. Figure 10, Chapter 16, page 171 gives you the basis for evaluating the difference between your sample and the population.

For example, if you know that the male-female ratio in your target population is 50-50, a sample with 45% males (a 5 percentage point difference) is not significantly discrepant unless the population is at least 1,500 and the sample is at least 600. However, a sample containing 30% males (a 20 percentage point difference) is significantly discrepant for populations as small as 150 and samples as small as 90. Larger populations or samples will result in dubious results because of such a wide divergence.

Be sure that any biases found in your sample will not seriously affect the results of your survey. For example, if you feel that your procedures are biased in some way, such as by omitting people with unlisted phone numbers, that your sample will seriously misrepresent your target population, you may undertake any of the following steps: (1) supplement with a door-to-door survey, and (2) acknowledge the bias in your report and specify how this bias may affect your results. Even those with unlisted telephone numbers can be contacted by randomly dialing the last four digits of a telephone number. Of course this procedure results in dialing many non-working numbers.

The kinds of variables that you will want to compare depend on the purpose of your survey and also on the statistics you can obtain for your target population. Sex, age, race, and geographic locations are the variables most frequently used. For example, suppose you were studying a sample of undergraduate college students, chosen from a target population of all undergraduates. If the topic had to do with the rules on who registered for classes first, class standing would be an important characteristic. In such a case it would be a good idea to present the class standing of the target population and compare that with the class standing of your sample in a table as in Figure 2. Note the difference column shows a one percentage point difference for each, well within the range of consistency for even large samples and populations.

Figure 2: Comparison of Target Population and Sample of Undergraduates, Citrus Univerity, Fall Semester 1995

	TARGET POPULATION (n=3,400) Percentage	SAMPLE POPULATION (n=338) Percentage	DIFFERENCE Percentage
Lower Division	53%	54%	-1
Upper Division	47%	46%	+1
Total	100%	100%	

Step 3.3: Deciding on a Method of Contact

Once the population and the sampling procedure have been determined, decide on how the respondents will be contacted. Three methods are possible: face-to-face interviews, telephone interviews, and mail questionnaires. Each method has its own particular strengths and limitations.

Figures 3.3 and 3.4 list the advantages and disadvantages of these types.

Informal Methods

In addition to the three formal methods, several less formal procedures for obtaining responses are also used. These include: handing out and collecting surveys at a meeting or in a class, placing the surveys at a check-in desk and asking respondents to complete the survey, or asking respondents to complete a questionnaire after they receive a service. Because you will be conducting surveys for community and government organizations, you may need to use one or a combination of these procedures to gather information.

The most important advantage to these informal procedures is that they are quicker and less expensive than a mail, face-to-face, or telephone survey. In some cases, they have the additional advantage of being taken more seriously by the respondent because the respondents are familiar with those administering the survey and the topic may be fresher in their thinking.

However, there are serious disadvantages that depend on the type of procedure to be used.

1. If the procedure is to leave a pile of questionnaires on a table with a sign asking individuals to complete the survey, the respondents may not accurately reflect the target population. Those respondents who have lots of free time or who have the most intense (usually unfavorable) feelings about the organization are most likely to respond.

2. The response rate may be poor. The example just cited is likely to result in a low response rate unless someone administering the survey encourages or even requires people to complete the questionnaire.

3. In meeting and classroom settings, the respondents may feel coerced to answer the questionnaire and therefore may not take it very seriously, or may give what they feel are the "correct" answers.

4. Never assume that it is easy to get permission to use one of these settings. You will always need to obtain the permission of the person in control of the setting (e.g., the teacher), and you may also need the approval of someone or some group higher in authority. For example,

any survey conducted in the Syracuse School District must be approved by a special committee in the district.

5. Never assume that the people asked to administer the surveys will take it as seriously as you do. You need to brief them thoroughly and monitor what they do by calling immediately before they are to administer the survey. Better yet, and if possible, ask if you can administer the survey for them.

Response Rate

One of the main differences among the three methods of contact is the different response rate which can be obtained from each. Face-to-face contact normally yields the largest number of completed surveys, telephone contact the second largest, and mail contact the least. The usual ranges of response rates for the three types of contact are shown in Figure 3.5.

The three methods of contact differ in other important respects besides response rate. Each of the three has particular advantages and disadvantages that you should consider in deciding which method of contact to use in your planned survey.

Figure 3.3:	Advantages of the Three Methods of Contacting Survey Respondents	
Face-to-Face	**Telephone**	**Mail**
Chance to stimulate subject's interest	Same as face-to-face	Low cost
Supportive responses by interviewer, producing better answers	Same as face-to-face	Respondent can decide when and where to complete it
Chance to do follow-up questions, clear up ambiguous answers, answer questions in the mind of respondent	Same as face-to-face	Respondent may feel more comfortable answering personal questions in private
Responses independent of literacy or physical disabilities of respondent	Same as face-to-face	Respondent may be less threatened by mail than by direct contact

Figure 3.4: Disadvantages of the Three Methods of Contacting Survey Respondents

Face-to-Face	Telephone	Mail
Very expensive; requires much time	Somewhat demanding of time	Respondent must take initiative to return questionnaire
Dependent on skill of interviewer	Same as face-to-face	Questionnaire may be dismissed as "junk mail" unless sent first class and accompanied by personal cover letter
Respondent may be more reluctant to answer personal questions	Respondent may easily terminate survey by hanging up	Respondent may ignore some questions

Figure 3.5: Expected Ranges of Response Rates

Face-to-face	75% - 90% response rate
Telephone	40% - 75% response rate
Mail	5% - 50% response rate

No matter which method of contact you use, you can do some things to increase the response rate:

• Keep the questionnaire short

• Make items easy to answer

• Use closed-choice questions

• Stimulate the interest or curiosity of the respondents

• Avoid embarrassing questions as much as possible

In any event, you must take into account an expected response rate when you decide how many members of the target population sample to contact. If you expect a 90% response rate, you will need to contact fewer individuals (for a given sample size) than if you expect a 10% response rate. The formula for estimating how many individuals to contact is to divide the desired sample size by the expected response rate, as the following formula indicates:

Required contacts   =   Desired sample size
selected from the   Expected response rate
sampling frame

For example, if you desire a sample size of 250, and you expect a response rate of 40%, the above formula (250/.40) tells you that you will need to contact 625 individuals.

Survey Ethics

In planning your survey, you need to be careful to respect the rights of the respondents. In most cases, surveys are conducted in such a way that the responses are anonymous, but in some cases the respondents may be directly identified or the responses can be traced to them. In any case, the survey should not be done without the informed consent of the subject, the protection of the subject's right or privacy, and the protection of the confidentiality of the data. It should also not create physical, psychological, sociological, or legal risks to the respondent. Frequently, approval has to be granted by an authorized agency. For example, at many universities, an Institutional Review Board must approve all surveys that may threaten rights or correct lists. Frequently, students in high school have to receive permission by the principal to carry out any survey. Any institution that is used as a site for a survey such as a school or prison must give formal permission for the implementation of the survey. Make sure you receive approval of someone in authority before conducting the survey.

Step 3.4: Creating the Questions

After determining the method of contacting the potential sample, your next step is to write the questions that you will use to gather your desired information. Keep the following principles in mind when creating questions:

1. Use simple and precise language with as few words as possible. This is frequently difficult to do because people attach different meaning to the same words. The KISS principle (keep it simple, stupid) is a good guide for questionnaire design.

2. Make sure the question and answer are logically consistent. For example, the following is poorly worded, *Do you live in the city or county? Yes ___ No ___.*

3. Do not waste time by asking questions that respondents are unqualified to answer. Surveys are widely used to predict the outcome of elections. When correctly done, they can be good predictors. The wording in such questions is not, *Who is going to win the upcoming election?*, something that respondents might answer but which typical respondents will not be competent to judge. Instead, respondents are asked, *Whom do you support in the upcoming election?*, a response, which, asked of an appropriate sample and properly analyzed, can give a good early indicator of election results.

4. Do not ask respondents to generalize too much about their behavior, especially over time. For example, suppose you want to estimate the frequency of seat belt wearing. You might be tempted to ask a question like, *How often do you wear seat belts?*
    ___ *Always* ___ *Sometimes* ___ *Never.*

    This asks respondents to generalize about terms that may be very inconsistently understood by different people. Another attractive, but defective question would be, *How often within the last month did you wear your seat belt?*

    Survey researchers have found that individuals make very unreliable estimates when asked to generalize about their past behavior. A better way to find out about, for example, seat belt wearing, is to ask the more specific question: *When you last drove your car, did you wear a seat belt?* ___ *Yes* ___ *No.*

    This question obtains unambiguous responses, and it asks respondents to report only their most recent behavior.

5. Avoid loaded or biased phrases in presenting the respondent with a question or statement. In case of controversial topics for which it is not

possible to offer an objective statement, use phrasing like the following, *Some people feel..., while others feel... What is your opinion?* Choose words carefully so as to minimize bias.

Closed-Choice Questions

This type of question limits the kinds of answers the respondent may give, requiring a choice of one or more of the answers provided by the question.

The major advantage of closed-choice questions is that the answers given by the subjects are comparable and limited in number, making tabulating and analyzing the data much easier. In addition, this type of question requires less skill and effort on the part of the interviewer and is easier for the subject to answer. The most serious drawback is that the closed-choice question may put words in the subjects' mouths by supplying answers they may not have thought of themselves. Most subjects do not want to admit that they have not heard of an issue, and they can conceal this fact by choosing one of the answers provided.

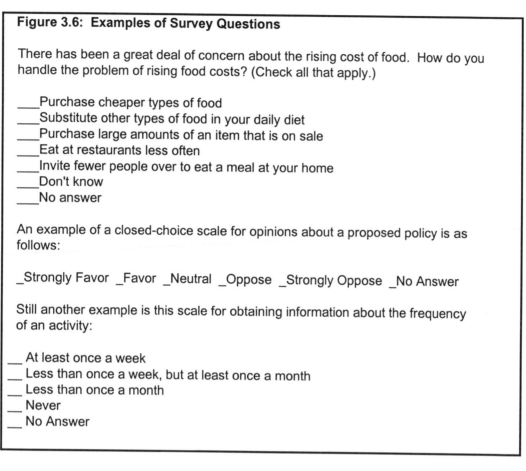

Figure 3.6: Examples of Survey Questions

There has been a great deal of concern about the rising cost of food. How do you handle the problem of rising food costs? (Check all that apply.)

___Purchase cheaper types of food
___Substitute other types of food in your daily diet
___Purchase large amounts of an item that is on sale
___Eat at restaurants less often
___Invite fewer people over to eat a meal at your home
___Don't know
___No answer

An example of a closed-choice scale for opinions about a proposed policy is as follows:

_Strongly Favor _Favor _Neutral _Oppose _Strongly Oppose _No Answer

Still another example is this scale for obtaining information about the frequency of an activity:

__ At least once a week
__ Less than once a week, but at least once a month
__ Less than once a month
__ Never
__ No Answer

Closed-choice questions may introduce bias, so construct them carefully. The wording and the ordering of questions, and the limiting of the choice of answers can all influence the respondents' replies. As an example, consider the question:

How much do you support clean air?

__Slightly __Moderately __Strongly

The question introduces bias in three ways: (1) it ignores the aspect of cost or priorities such as higher taxes for clean air vs. higher fuel and energy costs, (2) the choices given allow only positive responses, excluding both neutrality and opposition. Closed-choice questions must allow for an equal number of responses on both sides of any issue, (3) it does not include a choice for the failure of the respondent to answer. The same options for answering must indicate all possibilities, including the respondent's failure to answer. A better question would be:

41

This state is presently spending $1 million per year on improving air quality. How much money do you think the government should spend?

__Much More __More __Same __Less __Much Less __No Answer

Open-ended Questions

Open-ended questions are those that allow subjects to answer the questions without restrictions imposed by the wording. Responses to open-ended questions may be extremely difficult to classify. Open-ended questions, therefore, should be used only when they are clearly appropriate. An example of an appropriate open-ended question is: "What do you think are the main causes for the rising price of food?"

The most important advantage of the open-ended question is that the respondents can answer using their own reasoning and thinking patterns. In doing so, they may suggest new ideas. Another advantage is that open-ended questions do not select answers for respondents, which may be a problem with closed-choice questions. Also this type of question can provide a chance for respondents to "warm up" at the beginning of the interview or "cool down" at the end, when respondents may be asked if there is anything else they would like to add on the topic of the survey.

The major limitation to open-ended questions lies in the difficulty of making meaningful comparisons among respondents. Another problem is that interviewers require training to make sure that they conduct interviews properly. Finally, analyzing open-ended responses is more time-consuming than closed-choice responses. Whenever you decide to include open-ended questions, you must also include the specific procedures for coding the answers. Then you can make generalizations about the responses.

Step 3.5: Estimating the Costs and Time-Table of a Survey

Surveys and interviews can be costly and time consuming. Always weigh the costs of the research with the expected benefits that the information will provide. You should never assume that time spent in doing a survey is free. Although specifying exact costs and time tables is difficult until you have had extensive experience in conducting surveys and interviews, at least be aware of immediate costs. The following should be considered:

1. *Design.* How long does the survey design take to complete? What personnel costs will be incurred?

2. *Preparation.* What costs will be required to prepare and copy the questionnaire? How long will this take?

3. *Transportation.* How much does it cost to get to respondents for face-to-face interviews, including the costs of interviewers? How long will the interviewing take?

4. *Communication.* How much does the use of the telephone or mail cost? How much time must be allocated for telephoning or receiving mail responses?

5. *Analysis.* How much time does it take to count the responses or to enter the responses in a computer and run the computer program? What costs are required for tabulating, either by hand or by computer?

6. *Report preparation.* How much time does it take and what costs are involved (e.g, typing and copying) to prepare the report?

Below is an example of a budget and schedule for a proposed survey of students in a high school that is planned to begin on October 1.

Note some features of this particular project. No transportation or communication costs will be incurred, since the survey will be distributed to students through teachers in homerooms. Note the long time allowed for analysis of the data. Also note that while most tasks cannot start until the previous step is completed, the report preparation is planned to begin shortly before all the analysis has been accomplished. This is because the descriptions of the purpose of the survey and the procedures used in gathering the data can be written before the data analysis is finished. Even this simple survey will require more than $600 of resources and will take four months from the beginning until the report is completed.

Figure 3.7: Example of a Survey Time-Table

	Items	Cost	Starting Date	Completion Date
1.	*Design.* Labor. 10 hours X $10/hour: consulting with survey specialist	$100	10/1	10/31
2.	*Preparation.* Labor. 5 hours X $7/hour: typing.	$35	11/1	11/15
	Printing Costs.	$100		
3.	*Transportation.*	NA	11/15	11/15
4.	*Communication.*	NA	11/29	12/4
5.	*Analysis.* Labor. 20 hours X $7/hour: data entry & computer analysis.	$140	12/7	1/15
6.	*Report preparation.* Labor. 10 hours X $8/hour: editing.	$80	1/10	1/31
	Typing and reproduction	$150		
Total cost and time		$605	10/1	1/31

Step 3.6: Examining News Media Treatment of Surveys

The news media frequently report surveys relevant to public policy. When considering a published survey, keep in mind how well the news source reports on the procedures followed by the survey researchers. Steps 1-5 of this chapter are a good checklist to use in assessing a published survey. Some questions that should be asked of any published survey include the following:

44

- For what purpose was the survey conducted and for whom was it carried out? To what specific target population are the results to be generalized?

- What is the sample size, what is the confidence interval of the results, and how was the sample chosen?

- What evidence is provided that the sample reflects the target population?

- How were respondents contacted?

- What were the key questions and how were they worded?

- When was the survey completed, and how long did it take for the information to be gathered?

Chapter 4

Gathering Information from Knowledgeable People

YOUR GOAL

To identify and interview people who have specialized information on a public policy issue.

Introduction

Information about public policy issues gathered from library research and formal surveys often needs to be supplemented by information obtained from knowledgeable people, including:

- Government officials and their staff who make or administer laws

- Individuals and members of pressure groups who work to influence the public policy-making process

- Professional observers such as journalists and academic researchers

Because these people have a direct stake in public policy issues, they are good sources of information.

This chapter will describe what kinds of information are available from these sources, how to locate key people to interview, and how to obtain the most detailed and accurate information possible.

Step 4.1: Preparing for the Interview

Knowledgeable people can provide:

- Suggestions on material you might find in the library or derive from surveys. The expert may even have copies of studies for you to examine.

- Details on existing laws, administrative procedures, judicial decisions, and other information about activities leading to the making of public policies.

Knowledgeable people are more likely to help you if they are convinced that you are actively involved in the subject. For that reason, before directly contacting a knowledgeable individual, develop a basic knowledge of the subject and formulate a clear idea of the information you want to obtain.

In deciding what specific information you want to obtain, consider the following example. Suppose that you are interested in your school district's policy on closing school for bad weather. Here are some questions to ask: Who makes the final decision? Are there guidelines from the state about the factors that should be considered? How does the person making the decision get information about the weather conditions? Formulate questions you might ask with respect to the following:

Public policy: What relevant laws exist or are proposed? Which administrative agencies are responsible for implementing the laws? Have any courts made relevant judicial decisions? What has been the impact of the laws? What new laws are now being considered?

Societal problems: What are they? What studies exist about these problems? What studies are planned? How different will they be in the future?

Players: What are the key individuals, groups, and institutions responsible for the policy? Do they support or oppose the current policy? How much power do they have? How important is the issue to them?

Step 4.2: Locating Knowledgeable People to Interview

Once you have acquired basic background information about your public policy issue, and you have developed questions to ask, select the people you want to contact for more information. For example, your investigation of school policy on the cancellation of classes for bad weather might take you to the district office. You might want to contact the superintendent or an assistant superintendent. You might also want to talk to one of your teachers and an officer of the parent-teacher organization.

In deciding on which knowledgeable people you wish to contact, balance how easy it will be to contact the person with how much information the person is likely to give you. Generally, the people with the best information are the most difficult to contact. You may want to begin with someone whom you can easily contact and ask for suggestions and even an introduction to someone more knowledgeable.

From your background research, select the names of people and organizations that are mentioned in the news, books, and articles. You may also try to contact journalists and academic researchers who teach or who have published on the subject.

The telephone book is an essential tool for locating knowledgeable people, even if you do not have a specific name of an individual or organization. Telephone numbers of local, state, and federal government offices appear in the telephone book in a separate section, called "The Blue Pages." Non-government agencies are listed in the yellow pages under such headings as *"social service organizations," "environmental conservation and ecological organizations," "drug abuse and addiction information and treatment,"* and *"business and trade organizations."* Formal pressure groups may be listed in the yellow pages by subject or in the general (white pages) section by name.

If you have located the organization in the telephone book but do not know the name of a specific individual who can answer your questions, take the following steps: (1) call the main number, (2) identify yourself, (3) state the purpose of your call, and (4) ask for the name of someone who can provide information on your topic.

Step 4.3: Obtaining Detailed and Accurate Information

Once you have decided on the people and organizations you wish to contact, decide whether you will use the telephone, make a personal visit, write a letter, or e-mail. Initially, telephone to make sure that the person is willing and able to provide the information. Obtaining the information at the time of the initial telephone call would be most efficient. However, the interviewee may prefer a written request or a personal visit. The written request may be part of the organization's procedure. A personal visit, if possible, is always useful because you may be introduced to other people to interview and you may be able to study or even acquire written material. Always ask the people you interview to suggest others to be contacted. In addition, ask for written material.

Obtaining detailed and accurate information from a knowledgeable person requires you to be as informed as possible. We have already emphasized that you should have background information on the public policy issues in order to select the people you want to contact in the first place. Once you contact that person, the more specific the questions, the better.

Various types of people may give you biased information. Government officials will almost always provide you with the official viewpoint and will try to avoid controversy. As a result, the information will tend to be carefully worded and may be vague. People who are trying to influence government policy will explain things in ways that support their positions and self-interest. Journalists and academic researchers will claim they are objective, but they may also have a particular orientation. Also, the person you are talking to may not know the information, but may guess at it.

The best way to guard against possible bias is to ask the same question of two or more people that you know have different views on the public policy issue. If people on different sides of an issue give you the same information, you can have some confidence that the information is accurate. If you receive conflicting information, you may have to interview additional people, check other sources, or at least take into account the questionable nature of the information as you analyze your topic.

Step 4.4: Planning a Strategy to Contact and Influence Players and Knowledgeables

It takes time to obtain information from people and organizations. Therefore, develop a plan that will be completed over several weeks or even months. The plan might include the following:

1. Compile a list of knowledgeable experts as well as players that are concerned with your societal problem. Include people from universities, the business community, the government, and non-profit organizations. Obtain the address and telephone number of each person on the list. This may require initial telephone calls to make sure you have the correct address and name. This will take one to two weeks.

2. Send a letter as soon as you identify each person. Later in this chapter, there is advice on letter writing techniques.

3. Call each person one week after you have mailed the letter. Be prepared to ask some of your questions at this time, as well as to schedule a face-to-face meeting. Ask for material to be sent to you.

4. After your final contact, write a thank-you note including a statement of how your study is progressing.

5. Be prepared to make several contacts with those who provide you with the most useful information. The most important goal would be for them to agree to react to your written ideas. Make a personal visit if possible.

Adjust these actions as a result of the responses you receive. Most people you contact will be interested, but busy, so do everything you can to minimize the time and effort required for them to help you. Be accommodating with schedules and offer gratitude at every turn.

Outreach for Information

Figure 4.1 presents a model of how you should keep track of your contacts with knowledgeable people.

Figure 4.1 Sample contact Log

Date and Time	Contact Name and Title	Type(mail sent, mail recieved, phone call, interview, e-mail)	Description
3/28, 4:30pm	John Adams, DEC, Bottle Bill Expert	mail recieved	Recieved info about bottle law and effects on solid wastes
4/9, 2:30pm	Mike Smith, Resource Recovery Agency	mail recieved	Recieved info about recycling, composting, and landfills
4/18, 10:30am	Jim Jones, County Executive	mail recieved	Recieved a speech he gave about the need for waste management

Before writing a letter, make a list of your goals. What do you expect to gain from contacting this person? This will make writing the letter easier. Also, formulate questions ahead of time and write them down. Questions can be as specific as you wish, depending on the individual. Some examples of basic questions that can be asked of any player are:

- What policies exist that deal with your problem? How well do they work? Who is in charge of them?

- What studies have been done on your problem?

- Who are the key players and what is their position? How much power do they have? How important is this issue to them?

After formulating the questions, write the letter using the following format:

```
                                            John Smith
                                            Flint Hall Box 46
                                            Mt. Olympus Drive
                                            Syracuse, New York 13210
                                            May 26, 1997

Ms. Elizabeth Hollaran
Director, County Alcohol Abuse Prevention Program
100 East Main Street
Lancaster, State 44456

Dear Ms. Hollaran:

      I am a student at Syracuse University. For my public policy class
I am studying the problem of the abuse of alcohol by teenagers.

      I would greatly appreciate any information you have about the
following:

1.  What are the main causes of teenage alcohol abuse?

2.  What are the side effects caused by teenage alcohol abuse?

3.  Have any school-based programs been successful in curbing
    student drinking?

      Your agency has an outstanding reputation for combatting alcohol
abuse. I will be grateful for any information that you feel will help
me to develop a better understanding of the problem and possible
solutions.

                                            Respectfully,

                                            John Smith

                                            John Smith
```

Before sending the letter, read it carefully for typographical, grammatical, and spelling errors. Also, make sure the letter is neat. Always answer letters or requests for information promptly.

Step 4.5: Exploring the News Media as a Source of Experts

Radio and television news, talk shows, newspapers, and magazines all frequently publicize knowledgeable people who speak about societal problems. The fact that one of these individuals is quoted in a newspaper or appears on a talk show indicates that someone has judged this person to be either knowledgeable, a player, or both. However, do not make the mistake of assuming that people appearing in the news media are either the most knowledgeable or the most powerful. Luck and availability usually play a major role in their appearance.

If you do discover people from the news media whom you would like to interview, you can usually obtain their addresses and telephone numbers through the channels discussed in Step 4.2. In addition, you can call the reporter who wrote the story or the station that featured the speaker. In many cases, they will give you an address or send them your name.

Do not assume that individuals appearing in news media are so famous and have so many people seeking to contact them that they will not have time for you. In most cases, you will be able to get in touch with them directly. Even experts and players who are mentioned in the news media like to increase their audience.

Chapter 5

Describing the Problem and Identifying Its Causes

YOUR GOAL

To describe a societal problem and identify its causes.

Introduction

This chapter focuses on the analysis of a societal problem. You will be shown how to clearly describe the problem, support your assertion that the problem exists, identify the causes of the problem, and understand the existing public policies that attempt to deal with the problem. Without such analysis, you will be unable to find an effective solution to the problem.

To help you complete this task, the chapter is divided into six parts:

1. Describing the Societal Problem.
2. Providing Evidence of the Problem.
3. Identifying Underlying Causes of the Problem.
4. Describing the Current Policy.
5. Exploring the Role of Business and Non-Profit Organizations.
6. Examining the News Media's Discussion of Societal Problems.

Step 5.1: Describing the Societal Problem

A good description of a societal problem contains two ingredients: (1) a clear statement of the undesirable societal condition, including the specification of its geographical setting; and (2) an indication of how the condition threatens the attainment of the six societal goals discussed in Chapter 1.

As an example of a description of a problem, consider the steps you might take in selecting an acceptable topic. You might have read or heard people talking about "crime" as a problem. This sounds like a good topic, so you begin to do some research on the topic, consulting "crime" in book and article indexes at the library.

It soon becomes clear that "crime" consists of many different societal problems. Just a few examples include international terrorism, international drug trafficking, organized crime, murder, rape, mugging, robbery, vandalism, and so-called "hate crimes" against specific groups based on their race, religion, gender, or other characteristics.

Any one of these, as well as many other specific forms of crime, are the beginnings of a good description of a societal problem. Assume that you choose rape as the problem to be studied. You must also decide the setting in which to study rape. Although this is a problem in many different locations in the United States and throughout the world, you might discover that some rapes had recently been detected in your home community. Consequently, you might decide to select your local community as the geographical setting of the particular problem to be studied.

Upon further investigation, you find that "rape" is a serious problem, since it not only threatens good health and personal safety, as many crimes do, but it also threatens the freedom of choice of those who are victimized.

Step 5.2: Providing Evidence of the Problem

Since the very existence of a problem is likely to be the source of controversy and debate, you should attempt to provide a wide range of evidence on the existence and the extent of the problem.

You can obtain several different types of evidence. Each source and type has its particular strengths and weaknesses. These are outlined below. Evidence may include combinations of the following:

1.   Statistics showing change over time.   If you can locate appropriate statistics, this is one of the best forms of evidence of the existence of a problem, since a societal problem is often described as something getting worse over time.   One difficulty is that current statistics measuring the problem are often not available. Furthermore, some problems, such as those involving restrictions on freedom of expression, are difficult to measure with statistics.

2.   Statistics comparing different localities or different groups. Showing how one community, state, or nation is worse than comparable locations is also a good way to demonstrate the existence of a problem if appropriate statistics are available.

3.   Views of experts. This is a useful source of evidence for many reasons.   Expert interpretation of statistics is often more powerful evidence than statistics themselves. For example, while it is possible to measure air quality with great detail and sophistication, only expert interpretation of such measurement can be used as evidence that a problem exists.   Expert judgment is also important in showing the threats to goals such as freedom of expression or freedom of choice.

4.   Examples and case studies. These can be used to show detail about the nature of a problem and the effects on individuals and groups. In selecting case studies, be sure they are representative of a general situation, not unusual situations.

These four sources are generally available in books, articles, government documents, and similar publications, as described in Chapter 2. You may also, however, gather information yourself.

5.   You can gather information yourself through surveys (described in Chapter 3), interviews (described in Chapter 4), or observation. The advantage of doing it yourself is that the evidence can be tailored exactly to the problem and location you wish to study. The disadvantage of gathering information yourself is that it is costly and time-consuming. Even if you have the help of others, doing a good job of gathering evidence often requires careful planning, long hours of hard work, and sizable amounts of money.

Case Study

The specific societal problem we will attempt to show is that the curriculum and advising at American colleges does not adequately prepare undergraduates for a job. Evidence of the existence of the problem of the lack of job preparation by colleges can be found in several sources. The first item of evidence is a conclusion reported by Ernest L. Boyer in his book, *College: The Undergraduate Experience in America* (New York: Harper & Row, 1987). Boyer's study is based on a comprehensive investigation of the conditions of undergraduate education, including extensive site visits at a sample of 29 campuses and separate surveys of faculty members, undergraduates, twelfth-grade students, parents, and academic officials (Boyer xi-xvii).

Boyer says, "...we found the baccalaureate degree sharply divided between general and specialized education. Students overwhelmingly have come to view general education as an irritating interruption -- an annoying detour on their way to their degree. They all too often do not see how such requirements will help them get a job or live a life" (102).

Boyer concludes that although some colleges have made concessions to the desire on the part of undergraduates for job-related courses and advice, such response has come only grudgingly and has been inadequate. Boyer summarizes the views of many faculty when he reports that a history professor felt "deeply offended" by his college's policy of adding majors at "the whim" of local business interests (106). According to Boyer, "Many faculty members, especially those at liberal arts colleges, voiced the opinion that it is inappropriate for colleges to offer majors that are primarily 'vocational.'" Boyer quotes one science teacher who "declared that the college would be 'demeaned' if it offered programs that lead directly to a job" (108).

Boyer goes on to report that "at a small college in the Northwest, the faculty recently voted down a proposed major in computer science. 'It doesn't belong in the curriculum in the liberal arts. It's tied too closely to a job,' we were told" (108).

Another item of evidence, the graph, is shown in Figure 5.1 (next page). It indicates that out of three major forms of advising used by students -- vocational, academic, and financial -- vocational has been judged the least "adequate" or "highly adequate" by undergraduates surveyed by Ernest Boyer (53) in his study of undergraduate education.

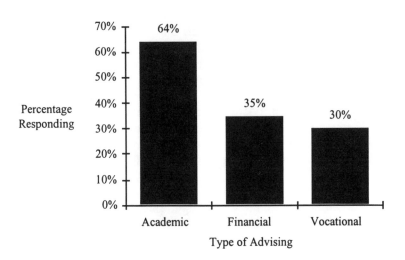

Figure 5.1: Undergraduates Give Vocational Advising the Lowest Ranking of the Three Types of Advising. (Percentage Responding "Adequate" or "Highly Adequate") 1984

Source: Boyer, Ernest. College: The Undergraduate Experience in America. New York: Harper & Row, 1987. p 53.

(Note: "Personal advising" was also on the list, but this form of advising was used by only 32% of respondents, and is therefore not included.)

Step 5.3: Identifying Underlying Causes of the Problem

In this step, you will identify the reasons for the underlying factors behind the problem you have described. While the search for social, economic, and political factors can require virtually unlimited amounts of research and never be fully completed, you should determine those factors most clearly contributing to the problem.

To illustrate, suppose you are confronted with the problem of a growing number of burglaries in a local community. You might identify as factors contributing to the increase in the number of burglaries:
- understaffed police force
- increased number of wealthy households
- inadequate security precautions

- stricter police enforcement in neighboring communities
- increased unemployment in the area
- increased illicit drug usage

Developing a list of possible causes is a good way to begin thinking about possible public policies for dealing with burglaries.

Case Study

The root cause of the problem of inadequate job preparation for undergraduates is the dominant faculty culture that views with suspicion anything that smacks of too much practicality. As Boyer points out, (108-109) there is much in the tradition of American and European universities that shows they have always been regarded as institutions imparting knowledge that has some practicality. Nevertheless, many faculty ignore this aspect of the tradition and concentrate instead on the aspect of "knowledge for the sake of knowledge" with little concern for the practicality of that knowledge.

Furthermore, faculty apparently prefer having students who are uncertain about their career goals. Fewer than half (47%) of faculty reported agreement with the following statement: "In my undergraduate courses I prefer teaching students with a clear idea of the career they will be taking," (Boyer 107).

This unwillingness of faculty to teach material that is applied is part of a larger problem, the denigration of teaching vis a vis research. The entire process of training young graduate students to become faculty, hiring, promotion, tenure, and salary decisions are all based on this fundamental set of values. At each step along the career path, a professor's research and other activities favored by others in the professor's discipline are rewarded much more highly than activities that service the undergraduates in the professor's classes.

In his book, *Scholarship Reconsidered*, (Princeton: Carnegie Foundation, 1990.), Boyer includes the results of a survey of faculty reporting that the largest change on their campuses in recent years has been to place a higher importance on research, at the expense of teaching and service (Boyer 31).

In addition to attitudes of faculty and the emphasis on research rather than teaching, colleges are faced with many students who have unrealistic expectations about the kinds of jobs they may have a reasonable chance to obtain. Many want to be sports broadcasters or TV anchors or high ranking government officials when there are few openings for such positions. Most want high paying jobs and assume that they only have the options of law, medicine, or engineering. They lack the life experiences and the maturity to see the relevance of general education and skill development to their vocational pursuits. These attitudes among students are in part caused by the negative attitudes of faculty toward "practical training" but students also contribute to the problem (Dr. John Smith, Professor of Policy Studies at Syracuse University, 13 June 1992).

Step 5.4: Describing the Current Policy

In this step, you will learn how to describe the essential features of one of the major current policies dealing with the social problem you identified in 5.1. As described in Chapter 1, there are three elements of any public policy:

- *Legislation*   to establish general guidelines

- *Administrative acts*   to establish rules and to distribute funds to put the law into practice

- *Judicial decisions*   to enforce the law and to interpret it in specific situations

Legislation includes both formal laws and agency regulations. For example, at the federal level, Congress establishes guidelines and approves the funding for government actions.

Administrative acts refer to all the activities that government agencies undertake to implement policies. A policy decision to increase police surveillance of roads in order to stop DWI requires many detailed decisions. These include the number of police cars, types of cars (marked or unmarked), and surveillance hours and locations. The legislation establishing the policy may require some administrative actions, but agencies almost always are allowed some freedom to make their own decisions in implementing policy.

There are three ways in which any given policy may require the outlay of funds:

- Direct cash outlays (e.g., unemployment checks)
- Purchases of goods or services (e.g., building a bridge)
- Provision of government services (e.g., police surveillance to check for DWI)

Judicial decisions take place when courts make judgments on specific cases. In some decisions, courts must interpret legislative or administrative acts. Legislative and administrative decisions or procedures may be declared unconstitutional if courts determine they violate the United States Constitution.

```
┌─────────────────────────────────────────────────────────────────┐
│                                                                   │
│  Figure 5.2:   Examples of Judicial Decisions Shaping Public Policy│
│                                                                   │
│  The Missouri Compromise, passed by Congress in 1820 to maintain  │
│  an equal number of free and slave states, was declared           │
│  unconstitutional in 1857 in Dred Scott v. Sanford.               │
│                                                                   │
│  Since the famous Supreme Court case of Miranda v. Arizona in     │
│  1966, police must advise a suspect of his rights at the time of  │
│  arrest.                                                           │
│                                                                   │
│  In 1974, in U.S. v. Nixon, the Supreme Court held that the       │
│  President must obey a judge's order to provide evidence needed    │
│  for a trial.                                                      │
│                                                                   │
└─────────────────────────────────────────────────────────────────┘
```

Figure 5.2:   Examples of Judicial Decisions Shaping Public Policy

The Missouri Compromise, passed by Congress in 1820 to maintain an equal number of free and slave states, was declared unconstitutional in 1857 in *Dred Scott v. Sanford*.

Since the famous Supreme Court case of *Miranda v. Arizona* in 1966, police must advise a suspect of his rights at the time of arrest.

In 1974, in *U.S. v. Nixon*, the Supreme Court held that the President must obey a judge's order to provide evidence needed for a trial.

Judicial decisions can increase or decrease the force of an existing law through the strength of the penalties imposed on violators of those laws. For example, stiffer penalties for DWI, as decided by judges, are part of a policy of cracking down on drunken driving.

When examining any policy, ask the following questions to determine what elements of government actions are involved:

- What legislation underlies the policy?

- What administrative acts have been undertaken to implement the policy? What funds have been expended to implement the policy?

- Has the policy been challenged in court? What kind of penalties have been given to violators of the law?

Information on the legislative, administrative, and judicial aspects of an existing policy can be obtained through library research and by interviewing knowledgeable people. Use the guidelines provided in Chapters 2 and 4 to obtain the information necessary to answer the questions above.

It would take years of study to acquire a comprehensive understanding of the role of public policies at the local, state and federal levels on any significant social problem. However, public policies are always contributing factors to the existing societal problem. Even the lack of legislation for a particular problem is itself a public policy. In examining the existing policies, you are automatically looking for the causes of the problem. Usually the policies are not the single cause or even the primary cause of a societal problem despite what some of the opponents of the policy may say. However, the policy itself needs to be considered when examining a public policy problem.

Step 5.5: Exploring the Role of Business and Non-Profit Organizations

While the government plays a major role in how we attempt to deal with societal conditions, other organizations are also extremely important. Two types of organizations other than the government that should be considered are businesses and non-profit organizations. Businesses influence societal conditions in both a positive and negative way. Business organizations that provide health services generally reduce poor health in our community. But, at the same time, other businesses market products such as alcohol and tobacco that threaten health.

Non-profit organizations exist to provide services either to special interest groups or to the public as a whole. The American Medical Association helps the medical profession support their interests while the Red Cross provides services such as blood banks and disaster relief to the public at large.

The solution to the complex societal conditions we all face usually requires assistance from the government (the "public sector"), business (the "private sector"), and the "non-profit" sector.

An example of the three sectors working together to address a societal problem is the movement to reduce drunk driving. Local government might step up law enforcement, bar owners might refuse to sell liquor to excessively intoxicated individuals, and Students Against Drunk Driving (SADD) might run an advertising campaign warning of the dangers of drinking and driving. When examining societal conditions, consider the role of private and non-profit organizations relative to conditions and how they would react to and be affected by public policies you would propose to address the conditions.

Step 5.6: Examining the News Media's Discussion of Societal Problems

The news media are a major source of information about societal problems. They provide more current information than books and articles found in the library. The major disadvantage is that news media, especially television, provide only rudimentary information and tend to emphasize the emotional appeal to the audience's fear, guilt, or greed.

Societal problems are rarely treated as systematically as the framework in this chapter. It is hard to find a background story, an editorial, or a talk show discussion that systematically defines a societal problem, provides evidence that the problem exists, and explores the causes of the problem. Usually, the emphasis is on how bad the problem is; frequently, the substitute for proof is the detailing of a few carefully chosen case studies. The discussions of societal problems that approximate the criteria provided in this chapter occur particularly on public television, some editorials, and exceptional op-ed articles.

Despite the weaknesses of the news media's treatment of any societal problem, a study of several discussions of a problem in different sources can often reveal a somewhat balanced picture. Keeping in mind the questions posed in this chapter, you may be able to develop a clear definition of the societal problem, an understanding of the evidence suggesting how extensive the problem is and where it exists, as well as the causes of the problem.

Chapter 6

Formulating a Position on
a Public Policy Issue

YOUR GOAL

To develop public policy alternatives and provide rationale for the
one you select.

Introduction

In this chapter, you will develop a public policy to deal with the
societal problem you analyzed in the previous chapter. This chapter is
divided into four steps. The first requires you to participate in an exercise
in which you will shape a policy affecting your grade in this course. By
participating in this exercise, you will experience the process through
which policy decisions are made. In the next step you will develop three
specific policy alternatives that you think will help to solve your societal
problems. That is followed by a step in which you will choose one of the
three alternatives. In the final step you will examine a discussion of public
policy alternatives in a newspaper article or editorial. You will be asked to
determine the degree to which the writer of the article uses an approach
consistent with the steps presented in this chapter.

Step 6.1: Evaluating the Grading Exercise and
Increasing Learning

One type of policy by which you as a student are greatly affected is
the grading policy operating in your class. How your teacher assigns
grades has a significant impact on your life. The following exercise not
only enables you to gain experience in the making of a policy that affects

you but also helps you to explore the role public and private interest goals play in shaping your behavior and the behavior of your class. The exercise gives you the opportunity to select how letter grades will be assigned to the numerical score you achieve on assignments and tests for this class. (Your teacher may choose to run this exercise as a simulation in which the results are not binding.)

In the exercise the class will select one of three pre-determined policies aimed at dealing with a societal problem considered to be significant by the authors of this book. The problem can be described as follows: "students do not learn as much as they should from this excellent book and course." Three grading policies are considered as remedies for this problem. It is assumed, for the purposes of this exercise, that all class members agree that there is a need for students to increase their level of learning in this course.

Overview

This exercise assumes that your teacher now marks according to a "Traditional System" in which letter grades are allocated in the following way:

Grade	Numerical Score
A	90 - 100
B	80 - 89
C	70 - 79
D	60 - 69
F	Below 60

After a period of class discussion, you will reach a decision as to which of the following three grading systems your class will use:

1. "Traditional System" as described above.

2. "Conservative System" in which students who receive the top 35% of the scores receive an A; the next 15% receive a B; the next 35% receive a C; the next 10% receive a D; and the remaining 5% receive an F.

3. "Socialist System" in which the students who receive the top 10% receive an A; the next 60% receive a B; the next 15% receive a C; the next 10% receive a D; and the remaining 5% receive an F.

NOTE: If either the Conservative or Socialist System is chosen, students who would be better off with the Traditional System will receive the grade designated under the Traditional System. The Conservative and Socialist Systems are subsidies to benefit different types of students. They cannot be used to penalize students who would be better off under the traditional system. In other words, these systems are designed to raise grades, they will not cause anyone to receive a lower grade.

By participating in this exercise, you will learn about the way in which what is perceived to be best for the individual (increased chance of higher grades), can conflict with what is perceived as best for the class as a whole (maximum learning for everyone). This conflict between self-interest and public interest is at the heart of all policy decisions. In addition, you will gain insight into other conditions surrounding the making of public policy such as conflict between minority and majority rights, respect for others, obstacles to a responsible and representative decision, freedom of choice, and equitable rewards for talent and hard work.

Procedures

The exercise should take two class periods. During the first period, you will discuss the pros and cons of the three options. A procedure for this discussion called The Somoan Circle can be used. It works as follows:

1. Five chairs will be placed at the front of the room.

2. You may speak only if you sit in one of the five chairs.

3. If you are in your regular seat, you may not speak.

4. Come up and sit in one of the chairs when you are ready to speak. You can remain in the chair if you think you might want to say something more. If, however, another classmate from the audience stands behind you, you must return to your regular seat until another seat is open.

5. You may say anything you want while you are in one of the five chairs as long as you respect the other members of the class sitting in the other chairs. Remember to state your views clearly and briefly. Don't ramble.

During the second period, your class will make a decision according to the following rules:

1. The final policy must be one of the Traditional, Conservative, or Socialist Systems.

2. If you fail to reach a decision by the end of the exercise, the Traditional System will stay in effect.

3. Your instructor will chair the class meeting.

4. The class can reach a decision in one of two ways:

    a. By unanimous agreement of everyone in the class selecting one of the three systems.

    OR

    b. If no unanimous agreement can be reached on one of the three systems, the class can decide on a voting procedure such as two-thirds majority, simple majority, or any other procedure. However, there must be unanimous agreement on the voting procedure.

5. Unruly behavior will result in the instructor requiring one minute of silence.

Debriefing

Once you have participated in the grading exercise, you should be able to explore the kinds of goals that motivated you, your classmates, and your instructor.

Possible public interest goals include the following:

1. Promoting more learning
2. Promoting equality
3. Creating a more just system
4. Maintaining order
5. Protecting majority rights
6. Protecting minority rights

Possible private interest goals include the following:

1. Less stress
2. Less work
3. Higher grades

The kinds of goals and questions raised by the grading exercise can be found in almost every public policy issue. All public policies benefit some segments of the society and harm others; just as the traditionalist system would result in lower grades for the less hardworking members of the class than would the socialist system. The conflict between majority and minority rights developed in the exercise is similar to the conflict between the majority and minority over voting rights and equality of opportunity in the United States. To the extent that the conservative and socialist systems are systems that provide subsidies to different groups, they raise questions similar to those raised about subsidies to farmers, tax credits to business, and tariffs on imports.

Disagreement among players in the grading exercise can also occur over means. Both sides may accept increased learning as a major goal; but those calling for a socialist system might argue that by reducing the stress over grades more learning would be achieved, while those calling for the traditionalist system would say that competition produces more learning.

You should also recognize in your behavior and the behavior of others the relative strength of public and private interests. You may be looking for a higher grade for yourself, but are putting your arguments in more public interest terms (e.g., claiming that the class would learn more). Even traditionalists, who have argued that they are only trying to preserve order, have been accused of trying to enjoy more personal satisfaction by raising the level of competition in the class.

A variety of analogies can be developed relating what happens in the grading exercise to past and current real world public policy issues. Look for the similarities and realize that policies of local, state, and federal governments will have a direct impact on goals important to you personally and to the society in which you live.

Step 6.2: Developing Public Policy Alternatives

Identifying possible policies that could make a significant impact on a societal problem is a critical task. In this section, you will need to identify three alternatives. Here are some suggestions on how to develop your ideas:

1. Review existing public policies as you did in Exercise 5.4. Do any show promise but need more funding or a slightly different application? Knowledge of the success or failure of a policy may lead you to come up with a new policy.

2. Look for public policies in other cities, states, or countries that might be applied to the geographical setting of your societal problem. If you find some, consider how you would adapt them as a policy alternative for you to consider.

3. Review the factors contributing to the problem listed in Exercise 5.3. Do those factors suggest possible policies? For example, the lack of effective locks on doors is a cause of crime in dormitories. Therefore, a policy to install new locks makes a great deal of sense.

4. Ask players as well as experts what they think would be effective policies. Study proposals made in legislatures, government reports, and academic studies.

In selecting the three alternatives, consider two criteria:

Effectiveness: select the policies most likely to have a major impact on reducing the societal problem.

Feasibility: select the policies most likely to be accepted by key players.

Unfortunately, policies that are high on one are often low on the other. For example, capital punishment for drug traffickers in the United States would probably be effective in reducing the use of illegal drugs; but, it would not be feasible because political opposition to such a law would be so great. Your three alternatives should be reasonable on both criteria. In general, feasibility is the more important criterion. It is usually easy to think of many extreme policies that would be effective, but they are useless because they are not feasaible. Policies that have a reasonable chance of being accepted (even if they are only partially effective) are generally the preferred alternatives.

Step 6.3: Choosing the Preferred Alternative

Once you have identified three alternatives, you will need to explain which of the three you prefer. Your choice must weigh the two criteria mentioned above -- effectiveness and feasibility. The example below may be helpful:

Figure 6.1:   Example of How to Weigh Feasibility and Effectiveness

Alternate Policies for Reducing DWI:

1. Establish a federal minimum drinking age of 21 years. (AGE)

2. Make all new cars sold have a feature where the driver must pass a breathalizer test in order to start the car. (TEST)

3. Make the consumption of alcohol illegal. (CONS)

| | | Feasibility | |
	High	Medium	Low
High		AGE	CONS
Effectiveness Medium		TEST	
Low			

The 21-year-old drinking limit (AGE) is the preferred choice because it is more feasible than the other two and is at least as effective as the other two. It has medium feasibility because many states dislike federal intrusion in this area. It is highly effective because it reduces the number of DWI arrests where it is the law. Testing (TEST) has a medium level of effectiveness, because it would slightly reduce the number of drunken drivers. Because of its extremely high cost, it is low on feasibility. Making consumption illegal (CONS) is high on effectiveness because it would reduce the number of drunk drivers. However, it is low on feasibility;

70

prohibition was already tried in this country and proved to be very unpopular.

Although you do not have to present the diagram in completing Step 6.3, you should use it to assess the three alternatives you consider. You will find it useful to draw it and place the three alternatives in the appropriate cells to help you develop your reasoning for selecting the preferred alternative.

Step 6.4: Examining the News Media's Treatment of Policy Proposals

The news media allows players and their audiences to express their views on preferred public policies. It may broadcast or report a policy proposal by a major player, such as the President or a member of Congress. The most elaborate presentations are usually found in the editorial pages of newspapers where space is provided for advocates.

A review of the editorial pages of newspapers will reveal that policies are not usually presented in the systematic manner suggested by Step 6.2 and 6.3. Rarely does a writer list three possible policy alternatives and argue in a balanced way why the preferred alternative is better on the basis of effectiveness and feasibility. More often, writers will provide only a simple proposal and provide one-sided support for it.

Chapter 7

Examining the Benefits and Costs of a Policy

YOUR GOAL

To identify and rank the benefits and costs of a policy.

Introduction

This chapter introduces you to the task of estimating, measuring, and ranking the expected benefits and costs of a policy if it is implemented. The previous chapter discussed formulating public policy. In that chapter you considered alternative policies to deal with a societal problem, and selected one of those alternatives. As that chapter indicated, a reasoned choice is based on your expectation of which of the alternatives will be most feasible and most effective. In this chapter you will make more careful estimates of the expected future effectiveness of policy. The next chapter will show you how to make a more systematic forecast of one of the benefits. Later chapters will deal with feasibility.

A careful consideration of a policy's effectiveness means making estimates of both the future desirable consequences of policy, called "benefits," and the future undesirable consequences of policy, called "costs." An effective policy is one which produces benefits that clearly outweigh its costs.

Examining a policy's benefits and costs should be done when formulating a policy. Weighing the benefits and costs of different policy alternatives helps you to decide which alternative is best from the standpoint of effectiveness. Once you have chosen a policy alternative, you can use its benefits and costs to convince others to support your policy.

In policy-making situations, policies that have been implemented in past years are studied to identify what benefits and costs they have actually produced. This process of studying the desirable and undesirable effects of a previously implemented policy is called "evaluation."

Evaluation is an essential task of public policy analysis because it measures the effectiveness of the policy selected. Unfortunately, it is a task not frequently carried out in a systematic way. Usually, policy-makers are so consumed in debating which policies to follow and how to implement them that they lack the time or energy to assess the impact of the policy itself. It is important that public policy analysts develop skills in evaluating policies.

Failure to evaluate policies hurts policy-making in several ways:

- Policies that do not work may be continued
- Policies that do work may be abandoned
- Potential lessons from our mistakes are lost
- Policy-makers are not held accountable for what they do

The skills you acquire in this chapter prepare you for beginning a policy evaluation study.

Step 7.1: Identifying Benefits

Benefits are consequences of a policy that you consider to be good for the society or some segment of it. For example, the primary benefits of mandatory seat belt laws are fewer fatalities and injuries to those involved in automobile accidents.

Benefits can be tangible, usually expressed in the form of dollars or other numbers. For example, seat belt laws might eventually reduce car insurance by an average of $30 to $50 per year, and decrease fatalities about 10%. Benefits can also be intangible and hard to measure concretely. For example, drivers and passengers may feel more secure wearing seat belts. Both tangible and intangible benefits are important to consider in evaluating an existing or proposed public policy.

Three sources of benefits are:

• The action itself

• The intended consequences of the policy

• The unintended consequences of the policy

The first category applies only when the policy itself represents a benefit. Intended and unintended consequences are less easy to identify. Intended consequences are, in effect, the goals of the policy. Unintended consequences are indirect results of the policy, changes produced that are not the goals of the policy, but are produced by the policy nevertheless.

Figure 7.1: Example of The Benefits of a Policy

The city government decides to take action against increased vandalism by youths. It implements a policy of hiring 100 youths to patrol the city parks. The benefits include:

• The action itself: the 100 jobs.

• An intended consequence of the policy: reduction of vandalism.

• An unintended consequence of the policy: increased enjoyment of the park by more people as the park's appearance is improved by the reduced vandalism.

The best way to assess the benefits of a policy is to use the six goals listed in Figure 1.1 which are derived from the phrase "life, liberty and the pursuit of happiness." Each of these goals may give you an idea of what benefits might occur for society as a result of this policy.

Step 7.2: Identifying Costs

Costs are consequences of a policy which are undesirable for either the society as a whole or some segment of it. For example, the primary costs of the mandatory seat belt laws are a loss of freedom of choice for drivers and passengers and more law enforcement expenditures.

Costs, like benefits, can be tangible, usually expressed in the form of dollars or other quantities. For example, a community's budget for additional law enforcement may increase by $10,000, a 2% increase. They can also be intangible and hard to measure concretely. For example, more hostile attitudes toward government may result from the seat belt requirement. Both tangible and intangible costs are important to consider.

Costs have the same three sources as benefits:

- The action itself

- The intended consequences of the policy

- The unintended consequences of the policy

Figure 7.2: Example of The Costs of a Policy

In taking the action of employing 100 youths to patrol the city parks, the city government will incur costs, in addition to the benefits cited in the section, "Identifying Benefits." The costs include:

- The action itself: the salary of the youths.

- An intended consequence: salary of additional staff to supervise the 100 new employees.

- An unintended consequence: more litter and increased wear and tear on the park from increased usage

---

In some cases, costs can be the opposite of originally forecast benefits. For example, because people are wearing seat belts, they may feel overly secure and drive more recklessly. A resulting cost may be increased traffic deaths instead of the expected reduction in traffic deaths.

Figure 7.3: Example of Costs Being Opposite of Planned Benefits

---

In the policy of hiring 100 youths to patrol the city parks, a planned benefit was reduction of vandalism in the parks. However, vandalism could increase because some of the hired youths could take advantage of their access to the park and increase the vandalism.

Costs should be examined relative to the six goals inherent in Jefferson's phrase "life, liberty and the pursuit of happiness." In general, the costs of some policies are often related to the loss of freedom of choice due to the required new behavior. Sometimes a loss of economic opportunity may be involved if the policy requires paying higher taxes or having additional costs of doing business.

Step 7.3: Comparing Benefits and Costs

Not all benefits and costs are equally important in choosing a preferred policy alternative. You must first decide which benefits and costs are more important than others before you can select one policy alternative over another. The only reasonable policy alternatives are those that have a good chance of resulting in more benefits than costs.

The following procedure is a simple method for calculating a benefit-cost ratio. Using it will help you choose among a set of alternatives. The first step is to assign a weight to each cost and benefit, based on its importance. Decide if you feel that the importance of each expected effect is "high," "medium," or "low." This judgment will not necessarily be accepted by others, because these are estimates about an uncertain future. Furthermore, people often differ strongly about the importance of different consequences. But if you are clear about your ranking, at least this will help you in your own analysis. Your ranking may also help you communicate clearly with others.

Assign a "high" rank to those benefits or costs that you believe will seriously affect several of the six goals. Assign a "moderate" rank to those benefits or costs that you estimate will have a slight effect on several of the six goals, or a moderate effect on one goal. Assign a "low" score to those benefits or costs that have just a slight effect on one or two of the goals.To help clarify the ranking, and to help reach a conclusion about the relative benefits and costs, translate the ranks into numbers as follows:

Ranking of Benefit or Cost	Numerical Score
High	3
Medium	2
Low	1

This helps show not only how each benefit or cost ranks, but also how to calculate the ratio of benefits to costs, as you have estimated them. The procedure is as follows: add the totals of all benefits. Then add the totals of all costs. Divide the benefit total by the cost total to obtain a benefit-cost ratio. If this ratio is greater than 1.0; the benefits outweigh the costs; the policy is worth pursuing. If the ratio is exactly 1.0 (the benefits exactly equals costs) or less than 1.0 (the costs outweigh the benefits), the policy is not worth pursuing.

Case Study

Consider a proposed policy of providing educational programs on crime prevention to members of residence halls in order to reduce larcenies. This policy has several benefits and costs, each listed below with the rankings assigned to each, depending on our assessment of whether their level of importance is "high," "medium," or "low."

Benefits	Score	Costs	Score
Reduction in larcenies	3	Staff costs	2
Increased personal safety	2	Printing	1
More work for staff	1	Loss of freedom	1

Of the three benefits, the most important is reduction in larcenies (ranked 3). The increased personal safety (ranked 2), while somewhat important, is ranked only moderate, because larcenies represent only a slight threat to personal safety. The benefit of increased work for staff (ranked 1) is only minor, since other important work could be found for the staff if they were not engaged in the educational program.

Payment for staff (ranked 2) is the most important cost, but is only moderately important, since most of the staff would be paid to do other things if not conducting the programs. The printing costs (ranked 1) are very low, less than $200. The loss of freedom (ranked 1) is also of only low importance because, although loss of freedom is very important, being required to sit through a crime-prevention session is a very minor restriction on freedom.

To estimate the benefit-cost ratio of this proposed policy, first add the scores of all the benefits (3+2+1=6), then add the scores of all the costs (2+1+1=4). Next divide the sum of the benefits by the sum of the costs (6/4=1.5). The resulting number (1.5 in this case) is the "benefit-cost ratio." When this ratio is greater than 1.0 (as it is in this case) this means that the estimated future benefits outweigh the estimated future costs of the proposed policy, and the policy is therefore worth pursuing. If this ratio is exactly 1.0, it indicates that the benefits and costs are exactly equal. If the ratio is less than 1.0, it indicates that the costs outweigh the benefits. In these latter two cases, the policy would not be worth pursuing.

Step 7.4: Analyzing Benefit-Cost Discussion in the News Media

The criticism presented on the one-sidedness of policy presentations also applies to the benefits and costs of a policy. Editorials and supporters of specific policies rarely look at both the costs and the benefits and discuss ways of systematically measuring each. They neither prioritize among the benefits and costs, nor seek to come up with a benefit-cost ratio. However, good journalists -- more often in the print media, though sometimes in the electronic media -- will attempt to present a view of both sides of an issue. It is useful to compare the positions of various commentators on a given policy in terms of the benefits and costs they identify and the weights they assign to them. A careful study of these views would lead to conclusions about the entire range of benefits and costs related to a specific policy proposal.

Chapter 8

Forecasting the Effect of a Policy

YOUR GOAL

Prepare a forcast of the impact of your policy on one of the societal conditions affected by your policy.

Introduction

Chapter 7 discussed how to identify and rank the benefits and costs that might result from the implementation of your proposed policy. By saying that a specific benefit or cost may result from a policy, you are actually making two informal forecasts: 1) what societal conditions will be in the absence of your policy; and 2) what societal conditions will be as a result of your policy. This chapter describes a more systematic method of making these forecasts.

Like the weather forecaster who attempts to tell you in the middle of the week what the weekend weather will be, the public policy analyst makes forecasts about what society will be like one year, two years, five years, or even farther in the future. As with weather forecasts, uncertainty surrounds forecasts of societal conditions. The farther into the future the prediction, the greater the uncertainty.

Forecasts for public policy, while oriented toward the future, are intended as the basis of immediate action. Those involved with public policy cannot wait one, two, or more years to see if a forecast turns out to be right or not. They must take the best forecasts possible, and rely on them to make current decisions about public policy. All decisions about public policy are made on the basis of some form of forecast, whether careful or sloppy, explicit or merely assumed.

Guidelines for Good Forecasting

Be clear with respect to what is being forecast, the time frame of the forecast, and the assumptions on which the forecast is based. Consider the following forecast statements that do not meet these criteria:

Figure 8.1: Imprecise Forecasts

- The U.S. National debt will increase.

- Homelessness will become a more serious problem in the United States.

- Traffic fatalities will continue to rise.

These forecasts can be improved by making them more precise with respect to the topic and the time frame of the forecast.

Figure 8.2: Precise Forecasts

- The U.S. National debt will increase by 3% in each of the next 5 years.

- The number of homeless people in the United States will increase by 5% in the next five years.

- Traffic fatalities will continue to rise by 3% in each of the next three years.

Cite academic or governmental authorities as the basis of your forecast. The best forecasts are those supported by governmental or academic studies from sources that are not only knowledgeable about the topic but also have no vested interest in the nature of the forecast. It is difficult to find such ideal sources, since many forecasters who are knowledgeable will have an interest in what the forecast says. You must take this into account when using someone else's forecast. One way to do this is to find several forecasts by experts on the issue and to consider all of their viewpoints.

Be clear about the reasoning behind your forecast. Whether or not you find authoritative sources to support your forecast, you are obligated to make clear your own reasoning for your forecast. Basically, you will make one of two types of forecasts:

- Things will continue as they have in the past. For example, "For each of the next five years, traffic fatalities in New York state will continue to rise 5% per year, because seat belt laws and speed limits will continue to be poorly enforced."

or

- Things will be different than what they have been in the past. For example, "The number of traffic deaths will decline by 5% per year over the next five years because drivers and passengers are increasing their use of seat belts."

Overview of Forecasting

The forecasting methods described in this chapter can be applied to any benefit or cost that you identified in Chapter 7. However, you need only apply it to the most important societal condition you have identified, that is, the most important societal condition that you expect to be improved by the policy you have proposed. Once you have decided what condition you will forecast, you will complete four steps:

1. List quantitative data that measure the societal condition for five time periods.

2. Identify the underlying factors affecting the variable that you are forecasting in order to make a baseline forecast, defined as a forecast of the societal condition assuming that your proposed policy is not implemented.

3. Make a policy forecast, defined as an adjusted baseline forecast that reflects what you anticipate the impact of your proposed policy will be.

4. Display the historical data, the baseline forecast, and the policy forecast on a graph.

Step 8.1: Listing Quantitative Data

Select one of the societal conditions that you believe will be improved by your proposed policy. This can be either a desirable societal condition that will be increased by your proposed policy, or an undesirable societal condition that will be decreased by your policy.

After deciding what key societal condition you want to forecast, obtain a quantitative indicator, or variable, that measures the condition for five time periods ending in the current year. For example, the benefit from a law requiring that air bags be placed in all cars might be measured by the variable of "traffic deaths per 100 million miles driven" for each of five years prior to the implementation of the law. The expectation is that this variable would show a decline after the implementation of the law. The effects of a policy to contain health care costs might be forecast by measuring per capita expenditure on health care, with an expectation that the recent increases in this variable would be slowed, if not reversed, by the policy.

Choose a variable for which you can obtain enough data for five recent time periods. Make sure that the variable is a reasonable measure of the societal condition you are forecasting.

In many cases, you will be unable to obtain data for the most recent year. Quantitative data is rarely available for the most recent years (or other time periods). In that case provide an estimate and give a rationale for that estimate. Indicate that the number is an estimate by placing an "E" next to the year. In some cases you will be able to find data for part of a year as the basis of your estimate. In other cases, your estimate will be based on your best judgment, including estimates of knowledgeable people.

Case Study

Consider a proposed policy to educate college dormitory residents about proper security measures in order to alleviate the societal problem of the number of larcenies in college dormitories.

The information provided below is based partially on information about a real university, which we will call Citrus University. It shows the absolute number of larcenies in resident halls, one of the more frequently reported campus crimes. This analysis, which was completed in 1998, lacked the statistics for 1998 so we estimated and provided a rationale.

Figure 8.3: Listing of Data on the Number of Larcenies in Residence Halls at Citrus University, 1994-1998.

Time Period	Number of Larcenies	Source or Rationale
1994	136	Citrus Univ. Security Dept. Annual Report, 1995
1995	123	Citrus Univ. Security Dept. Annual Report, 1996
1996	142	Citrus Univ. Security Dept. Annual Report, 1997
1997	126	Citrus Univ. Security Dept. Annual Report, 1998
1998e	136	Between January and June 1998, 68 larcenies were reported. The estimate was made for all of 1998 by doubling that number because about the same number of larcenies occur in each six-month period.

Step 8.2: Making a Baseline Forecast

Now that you have clearly measured the past trend of the variable, your next step is to make a "baseline forecast," defined as a forecast of the variable under the condition that your policy has not been implemented. Make a forecast for three time periods into the future. For example, if you have historical data on your trend line that shows change for each year, make forecasts for each of the next three years. If you have historical data for five-year periods, make a forecast for three five-year periods.

Making a baseline forecast requires completing the following:

1. Calculate the percent change.

2. Use your best judgment to decide what percent change you will use to make your forecast for each of the forecast periods.

3. Convert the forecast percent change into numerical forecasts for three time periods.

Calculating Percent Change

"Percent change" is the relative change of a variable from one time period to the next. It is calculated by subtracting the previous figure from the later figure, dividing this difference by the previous figure, then multiplying the result by 100. This procedure is summarized in the following formula:

$$\frac{\text{(Later figure - Previous figure)}}{\text{Previous figure}} \times 100 = \text{Percent Difference}$$

For example, the number of felonies in New York City was 637,451 in 1981, while the number dropped to 538,051 in 1984. The percent difference between 1981 and 1984 was -16%, or a decline of 16%.

$$\frac{\text{Total felonies(1984) - Total felonies(1981)}}{\text{Total felonies(1981)}} \times 100 = \text{Percent Difference}$$

$$\frac{538{,}051 - 637{,}451}{637{,}451} = \frac{-99{,}400}{637{,}451} = \quad -.1559 = \quad -16\%$$

Calculate the percent change between each year and the average percent change. Note that for the five time periods you will have four percent changes; the first percent change will be between the first and second time periods. See Chapter 16 for more information about percent change.

Choosing an Appropriate Percent Change

While each percent change, and the average percent change, can serve as the foundation for *reporting* your forecast, no formula exists for *making* a forecast. Rather, it must be based on your best judgment, using the knowledge you have acquired about the topic.

The easiest prediction is to say that whatever the average percent change has been over the previous five time periods, the same percent change will occur during the forecast period. If you do decide to use that reasoning, you are obligated to explain why you expect the same percent change to continue.

On the other hand, you may decide that the average percent change over the past five year period is not a good basis for your prediction. One reason would be that a steady trend up or down would produce a lower percent change figure than may be reasonable. In such a case, you may want to choose the percent change between the last two years or the average percent change for the last three years.

Second, consider special events or conditions. A major outside event or related societal condition such as a rise in prices or shift in the economic growth may produce a different percent change.

Third, the trend may be approaching an outer limit. For example, the literacy rate in a country may grow 3% a year if it is below 50%, but if literacy is approaching the 80% level, the annual change would probably slow down because the last group of individuals who are illiterate would be the most difficult to make literate.

A fourth set of key considerations are the demographic factors -- size and age of population. For instance, an older population would lead to lower crime rates and birthrates.

Finally, many societal conditions tend to be cyclical or self-correcting so that a period of major increase may be followed by a period of stabilization or decline. Slower economic growth in one or two years tends to be followed by somewhat faster economic growth the following years because people will eventually buy the products they wanted but did not buy in the earlier period.

Present your baseline forecast in a table using the format of Figure 8.4 which shows the historical figures, the historical percent change, and the forecast figures. The "number" is calculated by adding the number one plus your estimate of the percent change, and multiplying that amount by the previous figure. The 129 in Figure 8.4 for 1999f is obtained by adding -.05 plus 1 which equals .95 and multiplying the .95 to the 1998e figure, 136; 138 for 2000f is obtained by adding .07 plus 1 and multiplying 1.07 by the previous 1999f figure,129; 130 for 2001f is obtained by adding -.06 plus 1 which equals .94 and then multiplying .94 by the 2001f figure, 138. By adding 1 to the forecasted percent change, you create a factor that will raise or lower the total amount.

When you justify your forecasted percent change, clearly list each of the factors you consider which may lead to an increase or decrease of the variable in the future. The forecast you present will be, in fact, your judgments concerning the net result of all these factors. Also indicate how your baseline forecast is similar to, or differs from, the historical trend.

Case Study

The baseline forecast is that larcenies in residence halls will continue to show an inconsistent trend similar, on average, to the historical trend. While the historical average was slightly positive, averaging an increase of about 1% annually, the baseline forecast is slightly negative, averaging a decline of about 1% annually. Figure 8.4, below, shows the baseline forecast of residence hall larcenies for each of the next three years.

Figure 8.4.   Baseline Forecast of Larcenies in Citrus University Residence Halls

Time Period	Number	Percentage Change Historical		Calculations Percentage Change
1994	136	———		
1995	123	-9.6%	=	((123-136)/136)x100
1996	142	15.4%	=	((142-123)/123)x100
1997	126	-11.3%	=	((126-142)/142)x100
1998e	136	7.9%	=	((136-126)/126)x100

Average Historical Percentage Change (1994-1998e)= 0.6%

	Number	Forecast	Forecast Calculation
1999f	129	-5.0%	(-.05+1)=.95x136=
2000f	138	7.0%	(.07+1)=1.07x129=
2001f	130	-6.0%	(-.06+1)=.94x138=

The main factor leading to a decrease in the number of larcenies is student concern resulting from the history of high levels of larcenies in dormitories. The strength of this factor will vary from year to year. The main factor preventing the larcenies from dropping substantially is the continuation of poor economic conditions of the residents who live near the campus. Another factor keeping the number of larcenies high is the use of alcohol and other drugs by both students and neighboring residents.

In 1999 the larceny rate should decrease by 5% because of the residents' concerns from previous high levels. In addition, the poor economic conditions surrounding the campus, one of the main reasons for the larcenies, will ease somewhat as the city government is introducing an economic development project in the area. During the full three years of the forecast period a large number of neighboring residents will still be out of work, so the decline in larcenies will be quite modest. Throughout the forecast period the persistence of drug and alcohol use both on campus and in the surrounding community will also keep the number of larcenies at a troublesome level.

In 2000 the larceny rate will increase by 7% as the declines of the previous years produce complacency on the part of both students and security officials.

In 2001 the number of larcenies will decrease slightly, by 6%, as the increase in 2000 will again highlight the danger of larceny and produce somewhat greater attention to security.

Step 8.3: Making a Policy Forecast

After summarizing the historical trend and generating a baseline forecast, you will be ready to assess the impact of your proposed policy on the societal conditions that you have chosen to forecast. The policy that you have selected should have an impact on one or more of the factors included in the analysis you completed in Step 8.2. Thoroughly analyze the possible impact of the policy when deciding on your adjusted percent changes. As is the case with the baseline forecast, use your judgment, based on your knowledge about the topic, in order to make the forecast.

Compare the policy forecast with the baseline forecast. If it does not show that societal conditions will be better under conditions of your proposed policy, when compared to the baseline forecast, this means one of two things: either you have not correctly forecast the different societal conditions that will arise in the baseline and policy forecasts, or the policy you have proposed is ineffective. In the first case, you must re-do your forecasts; in the second case, you must propose a different policy.

When you have decided on the percent changes of your policy forecast, present the historical information, the baseline forecast, and the policy forecast in a table that can be used for ease of comparison. The percent change figures in the policy forecast can be used to produce forecast figures (as was done in the baseline forecast). Each figure is calculated by adding one plus the policy percent change, and multiplying that amount by the previous figure. The 122 in Figure 8.5 is obtained by adding -.10 plus 1 which is .9, and multiplying .9 to the previous figure, 136; 121 is obtained by adding -.01 plus 1 and multiplying .99 by the previous figure,122; 122 is obtained by adding .01 plus 1 and multiplying 1.01 by the previous figure,121. See Figure 8.5 for an example of such a table.

As with the baseline forecast, begin your discussion of the forecast with a comparison of the policy forecast with the historical trend. Also compare the policy forecast with the baseline forecast. Then list the factors most important in determining the rise or decline of the variable you are forecasting. Discuss the net effect of these factors on the variable you are forecasting.

Case Study

Figure 8.5 (below) shows the expected percent change and the resulting forecasts after the implementation of the proposed educational policy to sensitize students about dormitory crime. In contrast to the slight upward trend of the historical figures, and the slight decrease of the baseline forecast, the policy forecast shows a substantial downward trend, although this trend will be reversed in the third year.

Figure 8.5:		Policy Forecast of Security Awareness Program		
Time Period	Number	Baseline % Change	Policy % Change	Forecast Calculation
1994	136			
1995	123			
1996	142			
1997	126			
1998E	136			
1999F	122	-5.0%	-10.0%	(-.10+1)= .9x136
2000F	121	7.0%	-1.0%	(-.01+1)= .99x122
2001F	122	-6.0%	1.0%	(.01+1) = 1.01x121

The main factor leading to the policy forecast is the heightened awareness of dormitory residents produced by the educational program that will be carried out as part of the proposed policy; this awareness will be most effective only in the first year of the educational program. A long-term program of increased physical security will also lead to a decline in larcenies. Poor economic conditions in the surrounding neighborhood, as well as the use of alcohol and other drugs will keep the larcenies from declining to a lower level.

In 1999 this policy will produce a 10% reduction in larcenies. Not only will the program increase security awareness, but the publicity surrounding the initiation of the program will also make all students more conscious about taking proper security measures.

In 2000 the policy will still produce a slight additional decrease in larcenies. However, after the first year, students will become less careful about anti-theft procedures, and the factors that lead to larcenies will have greater effect.

In 2001, the slight decrease will be reversed. Students will become even less concerned about safety as the educational program becomes routine and as the lower level of larcenies leads to apathy about security. The continued decline of interest in following proper procedures will be balanced by increased efficiency of the physical security, resulting in only a slight increase in larcenies.

Step 8.4: Displaying Your Forecast

The tables and analysis that you have generated for the first three steps produce lots of numbers that are difficult to understand and interpret. To make your point more clearly, present your results so that people whom you may want to convince to support your policy can quickly understand the impact of your policy. This presentation will also make it easier for you to see the results of your analysis because it will enable you to compare the historical trend with the baseline and policy forecast. Precede the graph with a summary of the historical trends, the baseline forecast, and the policy forecast. See Chapter 16 for more information about presenting time series data with trend lines.

Case Study

Since 1994 the pattern of larcenies in dormitories at Citrus University has been very slightly upward, with sharp increases and decreases. Under the baseline forecast, the upward and downward trend of larcenies will continue, as in the past. If the policy of an educational program to alert dormitory residents to anti-larceny security measures is implemented, the forecast is for a downward trend in larcenies, although the decline will be slightly reversed in the third year of the policy as is demonstrated in Figure 8.6.

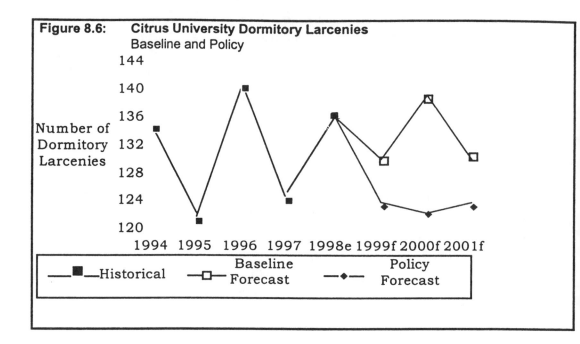

Figure 8.6:   Citrus University Dormitory Larcenies
Baseline and Policy

Step 8.5: Assessing Forecasts of Societal Conditions in the News Media

The news media frequently contain forecasts of societal conditions, such as unemployment, crime, or health care costs. However, many of these forecasts are imprecise and vague. Some explicit forecasts may be provided when an expert source is cited, but the reporting of forecasts is rarely as complete or systematic as this chapter requires.

Occasionally, historical trends are presented but rarely are explicit rationales for projections into the future provided. Even less often is an attempt made to project the consequence of a policy.

The news media, and many commentators on public policy, are also inclined to make implicit forecasts from the most recent event. For example, if unemployment increases in a month, the headline and discussion will tend to imply that this may be a pattern. Even if it does not, the inference made by most of the audience will be that the trend will continue in the most recent direction. Only occasionally, this tendency will be counter-balanced by discussions of why a particular figure may be temporary, and not indicative of a general trend.

Chapter 9

Forecasting Implementation with the Prince System

YOUR GOAL

To forecast the chances that a policy will be implemented.

Introduction

Good public policy ideas do not become policies without sufficient political support. A method for forecasting the chances that a policy will be implemented is the **Prince System.**

The Prince System, named after Niccolo Machiavelli's book, *The Prince*, is a technique for assessing the relative support or opposition of a public policy decision by various individuals, groups, and organizations. The Prince System requires the following:

1. Identify the **players** likely to have a direct or indirect impact on the decision.

2. Determine **issue position** - whether each player supports, opposes, or is neutral toward the decision.

3. Determine **power** - how effective each player is in blocking the decision, helping to make it happen, or otherwise affecting the implementation of a decision.

4. Determine **priority** - how important the decision is to each player.

5. Calculate the likelihood that the policy will be implemented.

You will learn how to perform each of these steps in this chapter and they are demonstrated by case studies.

Step 9.1: Describing the Policy to be Implemented

Begin by clearly describing the public policy you wish to see implemented. Using your preferred alternative developed in Chapter 6, 7, and 8, obtain information on the following:

1. The level of government at which the policy will be implemented: Is it local, state, federal, or international?

2. Legislative requirements: Does the policy require a new or revised law?

3. Administrative requirements: What agency will be primarily responsible?

4. Financial requirements: What funds, if any, are required?

5. Judicial decisions: How will the courts affect the policy? What cases could be brought to court resulting from the policy?

Be sure that you have defined a policy and not a goal. For example, "reducing unemployment" is a goal; "Spending $10 million of federal funds to provide job-training programs" is a policy.

Although the policy needs to be clearly described in order to forecast its implementation the exact details of its final formulation are not required. Frequently, policies are altered to gain the support needed for their approval. For instance, tax plans often begin with tax rates lower than those that eventually appear in the final version.

The following case study provides the description of a policy to deal with the problem of drug abuse in the community of Riverdale.

Case Study

The Riverdale Youth Bureau should create a court with teenagers as judges to try and sentence youths eighteen and under accused of buying, selling, and using drugs.

The Teen Court would sentence the offenders to rehabilitation, community service, and serving time on the Teen Court. This program will be controlled by the County Youth Bureau.

New legislation is not needed for implementation of the policy, and all administrative duties will be performed by the program director.

The court will be administered by a new staff person whose salary, expenses, and administrative costs will total $56,000.

No formal court action is required, but the District Attorney and the Town Justice would have to agree to allow this court to operate informally.

Step 9.2: Identifying the Players

Reasons for including a player are any of the following:

- The player has substantial legal authority.

- The player has political influence to promote or obstruct the decision. Players that can prevent the policy from being implemented are *veto players.*

- The player has formal or informal influence on a veto player.

Identifying the players to be considered is one of the most important steps in the Prince System. Including unimportant players or omitting important players can distort the analysis to the extent that it becomes useless.

A key to identifying the correct players is to consider the legislative, administrative, and judicial requirements of the policy. If the proposed policy involves monetary decisions, include players that have authority over the budget. If the proposed policy requires new or revised legislation, include the chief executive and the legislature. If the policy requires neither new funds nor new legislation, include the bureaucracies responsible for the policy and those that influence those bureaucracies. In addition to government officials in the executive and legislative branch, include players representing key interest groups.

To develop your list of players, begin by writing down all those that you think have some degree of influence on the policy. Next, reduce the list to between five and ten of those that you feel are essential.

The principal way to limit the number of players is to group individuals and organizations into collective players for the purpose of analysis. The process of grouping frequently appears arbitrary and can seriously affect the results if it is not done carefully. Guidelines that assist in grouping players to improve the accuracy of the analysis include the following:

- Group players having the same economic interests. In dealing with an environmental issue, for example, all private developers might be grouped together.

- Do not group players with veto power. This especially holds for governmental players. For example, for federal policy, never group the President and Congress.

- Do not group players if there is a disagreement among them or if their components have widely unequal power. For example, members of a city government could be combined as a single player if there were general agreement among them concerning the issue and if each person in the governing unit had approximately equal power. If there were disagreements, or if some members were much more powerful than others, it would be preferable to divide them into two (or more) players.

- Select a list of players that represents a reasonable picture of the overall power distribution. Do not include an excess of players that give one side unrealistic weight. If there is one collective player with an immense amount of power, that player should be divided into enough smaller players so that the total power is accurately reflected. For example, in dealing with the legislative branch, you might want to list the House of Representatives and the Senate as separate players rather than treat the Congress as a single player.

These guidelines are intentionally quite general. Your judgment in conducting the analysis is vital at every step. Rely on the Prince System as a way of organizing and guiding your analysis. Your success depends on becoming knowledgeable enough to select the right group of players.

In this case study, players are selected for the proposed Riverdale Teen Court from Step 9.1:

Case Study

1. James French, District Attorney of Riverdale
    His consent, with that of the judge, is necessary to create the court.

2. Joyce Zeno, County Youth Bureau
    She is responsible for approving youth related programs in the county.

3. K. Westcott, Deputy Director for Local Services in Division for Youth
    She has the authority to allocate funds for youth programs in the state.

4. J. McGrath, Chief of Riverdale Police
    The Chief would have to cooperate with the District Attorney and the Town Justice for the program to operate effectively.

5. Johanna Horton, Town Justice
    Her consent, along with that of the District Attorney, is necessary to create the court.

Step 9.3: Estimating Issue Position, Power, and Priority for Each Player

Issue Position is the current attitude of the player toward the policy. It is expressed as a number ranging from +5 to -5 to indicate levels of support or opposition. Assign +5 if the player is firmly in favor of the issue and is unlikely to change; a +4, +3, +2, or +1 indicate lower levels of firmness of the player's support; a neutral position is expressed as 0. Similarly, a -5 indicates firm opposition; a -4, -3, -2, or -1 indicate lower degrees of opposition. When estimating a player's issue position:

*   Read and listen to what the player says about the issue.

*   Estimate from the player's economic, social, or political standing what the player's position is likely to be on the basis of self-interest.

*   Look for differences among individuals and factions within groups and organizations. Look for inconsistencies in statements by individual members. If the contrasting positions seem evenly balanced, assign a 0 (neutral) issue position. If there seems a slight

positive or negative balance toward the issue, assign a +1 or -1 for the player's issue position.

Power is defined as the degree to which the player, relative to the other players, can directly or indirectly exert influence concerning the decision of policy implementation. A player's power is based on such factors as group size, wealth, physical resources, institutional authority, prestige, and political skill. Power is expressed as a number ranging from 1 to 5. Assign 1 if the player has a slight amount of power; a 2 if the player has more than minimum power; a 3 or 4 if the player has substantial power; a 5 if the player can veto or prevent the implementation of the policy with little or no interference by other players. When estimating a player's power:

- Ask if the player has the ability either to block or implement the policy.

- Determine if legal authority is a consideration.

- Consider whether a player has the ability to help or hinder the policy-making process.

- Determine, if need be, the player's wealth.

- Do not assume that a player, powerful on one set of issues, is necessarily powerful on all issues.

- Consider the allies and enemies of the player. Powerful allies increase power; powerful enemies diminish it.

Priority is defined as the importance that the player attaches to supporting or opposing the decision relative to all other decisions with which that player is concerned. Priority is expressed as a number ranging from 1 to 5. Assign 1 to indicate slight interest or concern for the issue regardless of the player's issue position and power. Assign 2 for those players with some concern, while a 3 and 4 indicate substantial concern. A 5 is reserved for those players that give their highest priority to the issue. When estimating priority:

- Determine the frequency and intensity with which the player makes public statements about the issue.

- From the player's social, political, and economic interest, determine the importance the player is likely to attach to the decision.

- Watch out for the fact that priority can be rapidly and substantially altered by external events and the intrusion of other issues.

- Remember that other issues and factors compete for the player's attention and, hence, priority.

As with selecting players, the assignment of issue position, power, and priority requires good information and a solid understanding of the financial, administrative, legislative and judicial factors affecting the policy. Systematic research can play an important role, but skillful assessment of existing conditions by knowledgeable and sensible observers is absolutely essential. Therefore, you have to be thoroughly familiar with the situation to provide accurate estimates on issue position, power, and priority. You should talk to other knowledgeable people and gather all available information on the reactions of individuals, groups, and organizations to the proposed policy. Refer to Chapters 2, 3, and 4 for a review of information-gathering skills.

Following are the estimates and justifications for the issue position, power, and priority for five players involved in the proposed Riverdale Teen Court:

Case Study

Player One: **James French**
Issue: +1   He feels that the Teen Court may be worth a try but he fears that high school students may not be morally developed enough to make these decisions about other teens.

Power: 5   His power is high because, as District Attorney, he has veto power and, his consent, with that of the judge, is necessary to create the court.

Priority: 1   His concern is with prosecuting all people who break the law, without partiality to any particular offenders. This proposal relates to only a small part of his responsibilities.

Player Two: **Joyce Zeno**
Issue: +4   She believes the Teen Court would be a refreshing new way to attack the drug problem.

| Power: | 5 | She has a lot of power because she could veto the program if she opposed it. Besides, she is director of the bureau that would implement the program. |

Power: 5   She has a lot of power because she could veto the program if she opposed it. Besides, she is director of the bureau that would implement the program.

Priority: 3   She gives the issue high priority because the decision, one way or another, will seriously affect her work. She recently wrote a letter to the editor of the newspaper expressing the need for community concern on the issue.

Player Three: K. Westcott

Issue: -2   She opposes the proposal because she favors the traditional court system that can impose stiffer penalties.

Power: 5   Her power is high because she allocates the funds for youth programs in New York State and can veto the project by withholding money.

Priority: 1   Her priority is low because the Teen Court is only one of the many youth programs in the state with which she deals.

Player Four: J. McGrath

Issue: -4   He opposes the program because he feels many teens will see this as just a way to avoid a jail sentence.

Power: 3   As police chief, McGrath has authority and influence in local government and the community and can indirectly affect the implementation of the Teen Court.

Priority: 3   He is concerned about the drug issue but has many other criminal issues with which to deal on his job.

Player Five: Johanna Horton

Issue: 0   Her issue position is neutral because she thinks that the penalties might not be stiff enough, but she does acknowledge that teen courts have been successful in other communities.

Power: 5   The implementation of the program depends on her cooperation as she has final jurisdiction over the offenders, giving her veto power.

Priority: 3   She gives moderate priority to the drug issue, but also is concerned with other crimes.

Step 9.4: Completing the Prince Chart and Calculating the Probability of the Policy being Accepted

After making estimates of issue position, power, and priority for each player, you can determine the probability that the policy will be implemented. The steps for estimating this probability are illustrated in the following case study, based on a proposed policy for the implementation of a Riverdale Teen Court.

Case Study

Figure 9.1: Prince Chart

POLICY: Implement a Teen Court in Riverdale
            (State in terms of **Desired Political Outcome**)

PLAYERS	ISSUE POSITION	X	POWER	X	PRIORITY	=	PRINCE SCORE
James French	+1	X	5	X	1	=	+5
Joyce Zeno	+4	X	5	X	3	=	+60
K. Westcott	-2	X	5	X	1	=	-10
J. McGrath	-4	X	3	X	3	=	-36
Johanna Horton	0	X	5	X	3	=	(15)

CALCULATION OF PROBABILITY:

Calculation 2:   Sum of all positive scores plus 1/2 neutral scores = 72.5
Calculation 3:   Sum of all scores ignoring signs and parentheses = 126
Calculation 4:   Probability of support = Calculation 2 ÷ Calculation 3
             = $\frac{72.5}{126}$ = .575 = (58%)

Calculation 1: Issue Position x Power x Priority = Prince Score
Multiply issue position, power, and priority for each player to determine the player's Prince Score. For example, James French in Figure 9.1 has an issue position of +1, a power of 5, and a priority of 1. The product of these three numbers is +5. If the issue position is 0, multiply just the power and priority to determine the player's Prince Score, and put a parenthesis around the score. For example, Johanna Horton has a 0 issue position, a power of 5, and priority of 3, leading to a Prince Score of (15). Make sure that you do not forget the negative signs, where appropriate.

Calculation 2: Sum of All Positive Scores Plus 1/2 Neutral Scores

Find the sum of all positive Prince Scores plus 1/2 the sum of all Prince Scores that are enclosed in parentheses (the neutral scores). In this case, the sum of all positive Prince Scores is 65 (James French is +5 and Joyce Zeno is +60). The neutral score is 15 for the Board of Trustees. Add 1/2 of 15 to the 65 for a total of 72.5 for this calculation.

Calculation 3: Sum of All Scores Ignoring Signs and Parentheses

Find the sum of all Prince Scores ignoring signs and parentheses. In this case, the sum of all scores is 126 (James French is 5, Joyce Zeno is 60, K. Westcott is 10, J. McGrath is 36, and Johanna Horton is 15).

Calculation 4: Probability of Support = Calculation 2 ÷ Calculation 3

Divide the number you found in Calculation 2 by the number you found in Calculation 3. In this case, it would be 72.5 divided by 126 which equals .575 or 58%. The calculation of the probability for the policy analyzed in the Prince Chart in Figure 9.1 indicates that there is a 58% chance that the teen court will be implemented. This indicates it is uncertain whether the policy will be implemented.

Figure 9.2: Interpretation of Probability

100%	Certain to be implemented. In case of 100% agreement on a policy then there is no public policy issue.
60% - 99%	Likely to be implemented
40% - 59%	Uncertain. Likely to be disputed without resolution.
1% - 39%	Unlikely to be implemented. Likely to be killed as a proposal.
0%	Never will be implemented. In case of 0% support of a proposal, there is no public policy issue.

Step 9.5: Forecasting Policy Implementation in the News Media

The news media almost never make forecasts concerning whether or not a policy will be implemented. Occasionally, players and experts are asked to make forecasts that are then published. The news media will report which players are supporting proposed policies, but the most powerful players usually have issue positions which are not firm. These players will take pains to keep their options open or, if they have reached a decision, not to make their views public. As a result, it is difficult to get clear information on the issue position, power, and priority of players as well as on the general likelihood of a policy proposal from the media.

Chapter 10

Developing Political Strategies

YOUR GOAL

To develop strategies for affecting the chances that a policy will be implemented.

Introduction

In Chapter 9, you learned how to forecast the likelihood that a proposed policy would be implemented. That analysis is based on the information you have about political support and opposition at a given time. However, political support and opposition can change constantly as a result of elections, new social conditions, or even accidents. For example, the support for large government expenditures on drug education may suddenly increase when an athlete, actor, or other well-known figure dies from a drug overdose.

Among the main sources of change are the actions different players take to support or oppose a policy. For example, Mothers Against Drunk Driving (MADD) often threatens to oppose legislators seeking re-election if they do not vote for strong DWI laws. These actions are called strategies because they are taken to achieve a specific goal: to increase or decrease the likelihood that a policy will be implemented.

In this chapter, you will learn how to formulate a strategy using the information you gathered in Chapter 9. The case studies that began in Chapter 9 will be extended into this chapter.

Step 10.1: Selecting a Player for Developing a Strategy

The first step in developing a strategy is to determine whether or not you want a policy implemented or defeated. You can make a decision on the basis of your own feelings about the policy or select a position based on other considerations.

The exercises in this chapter require you to develop a strategy on behalf of one of the players in your Prince analysis from Chapter 9. Select a player that has a firm issue position and high priority. Do not select a player unless it has a score of at least 3 on both factors. The reason for this is that players with scores of less than a 3 on issue position and priority are not likely to pursue a strategy since they are open to changing their position and do not care enough to take strong action.

Your selection of a player may also depend upon your knowledge of the player's power. Select a player with a significant amount of power because such a player will have more strategies available.

The following case study shows an example of player selection for the proposed policy discussed in Chapter 9.

Case Study

For the proposed Riverdale Teen Court, the player chosen is Ms. Joyce Zeno. There are many reasons to choose Ms. Zeno: Ms. Zeno has a lot of power (5) in her position as Director of the Youth Bureau. Thus, she can choose from a wide variety of strategies. Her issue position is a +4 which means she has a firm position in support of the policy. She also gives the Teen Court policy a moderate priority (3), so she will be willing to work hard to change the positions of others to increase support for the Teen Court.

Step 10.2: Constructing a Prince Political Map

As an aid in developing a strategy based on the information provided in the Prince Chart, construct a Prince Political Map. This is a display of the information you have in the Prince Chart so that you can see where you would like players to be in order to achieve your goal. Location on the vertical axis is determined by the player's issue position. Location on the horizontal axis is determined by multiplying the player's power and priority.

Using the numbers developed in 9.3, the following case study presents a Prince Map.

Case Study

The following is the Prince Political Map for the proposed Riverdale Teen Court based on the Prince Chart from Chapter 9:

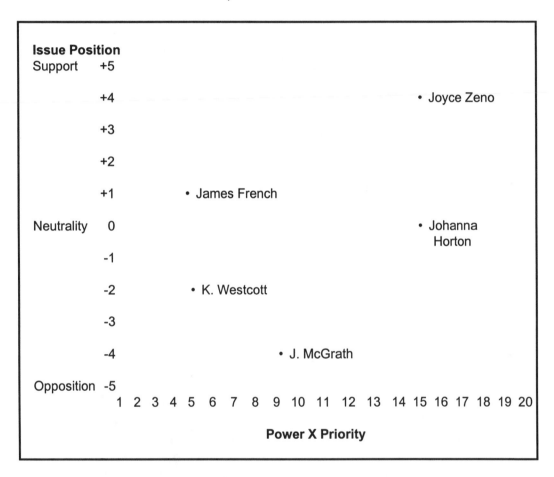

Issue Position		
Support	+5	
	+4	• Joyce Zeno
	+3	
	+2	
	+1	• James French
Neutrality	0	• Johanna Horton
	-1	
	-2	• K. Westcott
	-3	
	-4	• J. McGrath
Opposition	-5	

1 2 3 4 5 6 7 8 9 10 11 12 13 14 15 16 17 18 19 20

Power X Priority

Step 10.3: Describing a Political Strategy

You are now ready to select specific actions to increase the support for your player's position on the issue. Your goal is to take actions that move players on the Prince Map so the situation becomes more favorable to you.

- If your goal is to increase the chances that the policy will be implemented, move as many players as possible toward the upper right-hand corner of the map.

- If your goal is to reduce the chances that the policy will be implemented, move as many players as possible toward the lower right-hand corner of the map.

- For players that have a firm position opposite to yours, move them as far toward the left-hand side of the map as possible.

Your strategy need not cause a complete shift; any movement in the directions indicated above is an improvement. To move players around on the Prince Political Map, four basic strategy goals are available:

- Add new players that will occupy the position you want on the map or delete players that now occupy positions on the map that are undesirable from your point of view.

- Change the issue position of players.

- Change the power of players.

- Change the priority of players.

In planning your strategic action, it is important to distinguish between strategy goals and the strategies to achieve these goals. Strategy goals include various desired changes that would alter probability as you wish it to be altered. Strategies are the specific actions you decide to take to achieve your goals. For example, a goal might be to raise players' priorities. The strategy to achieve that goal might be to issue a statement to the news media that will raise the players' priority levels.

Strategies for Achieving Strategy Goals

1. *Add new players or delete existing players.*
   This strategy goal can radically alter the chances of a decision, but it is very difficult to implement. For any public policy issue, players in the game are not likely to leave. The exceptions are politicians who lose elections and individuals with health or personal problems. New players might be added as a result of elections, and campaigning actively for certain candidates would be one way to achieve that

strategy goal. Adding new players can also be accomplished by creating new organizations. For example, various students who support a particular school policy change could establish a formal organization as a strategy.

2. *Change the issue position of players.*
   This strategy goal is the most frequently sought. Its effectiveness depends on the power and skill of the player using it and the attitudes of the target players. There are four basic ways to change a player's issue position:

- Make specific promises to do something in exchange for a shift in issue position. In legislatures, this is called logrolling; when one legislator supports one bill in order to win another legislator's support on another issue. Campaign contributors promise money in exchange for support promised by candidates. This often works best when you work with special interest groups on a strategy.

- Redefine the policy to accommodate the interests of those opposed without sacrificing its essential ingredients. This is usually called compromise; it is found in all kinds of decision-making political bodies.

- Make threats to do something unpleasant if the player does not shift position. Lobbyists and legislators sometimes resort to threats if promises do not work.

- Make arguments that use facts and emotional appeals to change the player's mind. This is a form of lobbying. This strategy is always necessary, but it cannot be used by itself. It must be accompanied by other strategies in order to work.

The four ways to change issue positions of players are listed in the order of general effectiveness. Promises and compromise are less costly than threats to the player pursuing the strategy. Threats are costly because they can backfire. The player might stick to its own position even more firmly. Threats, therefore, should be used only as a last resort. Arguments are made by all players all the time; as a result they have limited effectiveness. Although arguments are a necessary ingredient to any strategy, they never work by themselves.

The firmer a player's issue position, the more difficult it is to move that player. If the player is on your side, a firm position indicates a reliable ally. If the player is on the opposite side, firmness is a measure of how difficult it will be to get your strategy to work. If you move a player that is -5 to a +1, the chances of success are increased more than if you move a -1 player to a +1. However, it is easier to move the -1 player to a +1. You often have to choose between a large chance of a small gain against a small chance of a large gain.

3. *Change the power of yourself and other players.*
   Power comes from a variety of sources, including:

- Appointed or elected position in the policy-making process

- Wealth

- Organizational size and cohesion

- Reputation for knowledge

- Number and importance of friends and enemies

  Increasing the power of your allies and decreasing the power of your opponents takes a long time and a great deal of work. However, there may be no other choice. Remember, you obtain maximum results from power strategies if you direct them at players with firm positions and high priority.

4. *Change the priority of other players.*
   Priority strategies fall into three categories:

- Trying to raise priority by creating events that generate publicity or distributing information on the issue. Issuing a news release or writing a public service announcement are ways to do this.

- Trying to lower priority by keeping the issue quiet or generating other issues that take your issue out of the spotlight.

- Trying to raise or lower priority by compromising or redefining a proposed policy.

Use publicity with care. It is not always to your advantage to raise the priority of all players. If your opponents have high priority and those who support you have lower priority, raising priority will improve your situation. However, if your supporters already have high priority and your opponents do not, raising priority will hurt you. In fact, in this case, your strategy goal should be to lower priority among players.

To formulate an effective political strategy, once you have decided on the player you wish to represent, examine the Prince Political Map and do the following:

- Decide on which players you wish to concentrate.

- Consider the four types of strategy goals just presented.

- Select a strategy that will move players in the direction you want.

Make sure that the player you represent can actually carry out the strategy. Spell out the specific steps that might be taken to execute your strategy. Some examples of specific steps that you could take are lobbying or issuing press releases.

The following case study explores an example of a strategy:

Case Study

For the proposed Riverdale Teen Court, Joyce Zeno will try to decrease opposition to the policy by using the strategy of compromise. She recognizes James French's concern that teens may not be morally developed enough to make such mature decisions. She will propose creating an advisory board to review the decisions made by the court. This board would consist of herself, Mr. French, and members of the community who are interested in and knowledgeable about the issue.

Step 10.4: Assessing the Impact of the Proposed Strategy

Once you have described your strategy, discuss its impact. Forecast how each of the players on the Prince Political Map will be affected by the strategies. Examine the effects of your strategy on each player even if the strategy is designed to work primarily on only one. Remember that the players are constantly keeping track of one another; there will be some indirect effects of any strategy you pursue.

To assess the impact of your strategy:

1. Provide a summary of what changes you expect in issue position, power, and priority as a result of your strategy.

2. Draw arrows on the Prince Political Map prepared in your original analysis showing how players will move as a result of your strategy.

3. Recalculate a new Prince Chart with the changed issue position, power, and priority scores.

Remember also that different strategies have different effects on different players. Promises, compromises, threats, and arguments will change only the issue position of players. Increasing publicity through such actions as petitions, pickets, and demonstrations will raise priority, but may not change either issue position or power. Most power strategies take a long time to be effective and may affect several players.

The following describes the impact of the strategy proposed in Step 10.3 on the players involved with the proposed Riverdale Teen Court. An "S" indicates that the score remained the same.

Case Study

Player	Original Score	New Score	Reasons
James French	Position +1	+3	His main reservation was the possibility that teens might not make responsible decisions. If there is an adult board, he is willing to give the policy more of a chance.
	Power 5	S	
	Priority 1	S	
K. Westcott	Position -2	S	The compromise does not change her opposition. She still favors the traditional court system.
	Power 5	S	
	Priority 1	S	

J. McGrath	Position	-4	-2	He was afraid the teens would just see the Teen Court as a way to avoid a jail sentence. His opposition to the proposal is less as he thinks an advisory board may be able to monitor this, although he still has reservations.
	Power	3	S	
	Priority	3	S	
Johanna Horton	Position	0	+1	She feels that the board could monitor the penalties and make sure they are stiff enough. Thus, she gives slight support to the policy. Her priority declines because she is no longer concerned about negative effects of the policy.
	Power	5	S	
	Priority	3	2	

The following shows the new Prince Chart based on the results of the strategy:

Players	Issue Position -5 to +5	X	Power 1 to 5	X	Priority 1 to 5	=	Player's Prince Score
James French	+3	X	5	X	1	=	+15
Joyce Zeno	+4	X	5	X	3	=	+60
K. Westcott	-2	X	5	X	1	=	-10
J. McGrath	-2	X	3	X	3	=	-18
Johanna Horton	+1	X	5	X	2	=	+10

Calculation of Probability

Calculation 2: Sum of all positive scores plus 1/2 neutral scores = 85

Calculation 3: Sum of all scores ignoring signs and parentheses = 113

Calculation 4: Probability = Calculation 2 divided by Calculation 3

$$= \frac{85}{113} = .75 \times 100 = 75\%$$

111

The following Prince Political Map forecasts the effect of the proposed strategy with arrows:

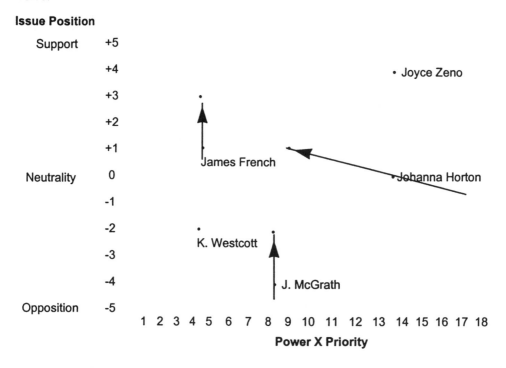

Step 10.5: Discussing Strategies for Policy Implementation from the News Media

The strategies considered by players to deal with a proposed policy are rarely described in the news media because timing and surprise are often key ingredients. An occasional source of this information is the news analysis television or radio programs where observers are asked to speculate on the strategies that might be followed by a given player. Another source would be the strategies followed by interest groups that adopt a public stance on an issue.

Chapter 11

Preparing a Policy Briefing Paper

YOUR GOAL

To create a clear, concise and sound policy proposal based on the concepts presented in Chapters 1-10.

Introduction

This chapter provides guidelines for writing a paper that will integrate the work you have completed in Chapters 1-10. The paper, which should be no more than 2,000 words, can be used to present your views to players in a way that will gain both their attention and respect. The format presented in this chapter is widely used by top leaders in business, government, and the not-profit sector.

Start the paper with a one-page **executive summary** that describes each of the other sections of the paper. It moves to a **formulation** section where the problem is clearly identified and the causes contributing to the problem succintly discussed. The next section, **implementation,** discusses what needs to be done to implement the policy both administratively and politically. The final section, **evaluation**, discusses your plans for evaluating the policy after it has been implemented.

The guidelines presented on the next few pages can be used without having done the exercises in Chapters 1-10, but if you have done those chapters, your first step is to review your work, particularly in Chapters 5-10.

In the five previous chapters, you completed a series of steps that began with identifying a societal problem, proposing a public policy to deal with that problem, forecasting the impact of that policy, and analyzing the chances of the policy's being implemented. The critical stage in the analysis was the selection of the policy alternative.

In selecting the policy in Step 6.3, you were asked to weigh the benefits, costs, and political feasibility of your proposed policy against the benefits, costs, and political feasibility of alternative policies. Because you had not conducted the analysis required in Chapters 7, 8, 9 and 10 prior to Step 6.3, your initial judgment was not as informed as it is now.

As a result of your additional knowledge and analysis, you should now reach one of the following conclusions:

1. Your policy as stated was the best among the alternatives you suggested.

2. Your policy was on the right track, but it needs revision because of uncertainty about its benefits and costs (covered in Chapter 7) or because of questions about its political feasibility (covered in Chapters 9 and 10).

3. One of the other policy alternatives considered in Chapter 6 would be better than the one you have been analyzing.

4. A completely new alternative would be preferable.

Once you have reviewed your previous work you are ready to write each of the four sections described below. In writing the paper, keep in mind for your audience at least one specific player in order to decide on how much detail and background to include. The player should be an official in the administration, the legislature, or a lobbying group. Although your paper may also be addressed to broader audiences such as readers of the newspaper or influential members of the community, keep at least one specific player in mind when drafting your paper.

SUMMARY

The purpose of the summary is to give the reader an idea of what is contained in the paper. Although it is the first section of the paper, it should be written last, using material form the rest of the paper. The summary should follow the organization of the paper exactly. In fact, some of the same sentences that appear in the summary may be used to introduce each section of the paper. The summary should be

comprehensive enough so that it can be understood without reading the remainder of the report.
(Suggested length: 300 words)

FORMULATION

The formulation section should do the following:

(1) Identify a societal problem you seek to alleviate through your policy. Provide evidence that demonstrates the extent of the problem.

(2) Discuss the social, economic, and political factors that contribute to the problem you have identified.

(3) Discuss at least three specific public policy proposals that might deal with the problem. Select and justify the one you think will be the most effective and politically feasible. Your policy can require local, state, or federal action by a government agency. All three proposals should be based on action in the same geographical jurisdiction.

(Suggested length: 300 to 600 words)

IMPLEMENTATION

Implementation means putting the public policy into effect. To assess whether a policy will be implemented, answer these questions:

(1) What are the financial requirements of the policy? What will be the source of any required funds? Some public policies require very little government spending while others require a great deal. Although you cannot specify the exact amount of money required, you can give a general estimate. If finances are significant, indicate what government agency will provide the funds.

(2) What are the legislative requirements? Some public policies require legislation; others just require an administrative decision. Indicate whether and at which level (local, state, or federal) legislation is required.

(3)What are the required administrative operations? "Administrative operations" are activities officials perform on a routine basis. Some policies require such activities; others do not.

(4) What are the chances the policy will be implemented? Discuss the degree to which the policy is supported and opposed by players involved in making policy. "Players" are leaders and individuals who will directly or indirectly determine the formulation and actual implementation of the policy. They include those formally responsible for making policy, those who influence policy makers, and those who will be able to affect the way the policy is implemented. Assess the relative strengths of the supporting and opposing forces to forecast the likelihood that the policy will be maintained or implemented.

The implementation section of the paper will demonstrate your understanding of the political realities surrounding public policy decisions. It is not enough to identify a good public policy alternative; you must also assess the chances that the policy will be implemented. Although your analysis will not be completely useless if you choose a policy that has only a small chance of being adopted, failing to recognize the odds against a policy will seriously damage your credibility in the eyes of those who evaluate your arguments. When discussing chances of implementation, indicate under what conditions and strategies the chances might increase or decrease.
(Suggested length: 300 to 600 words.)

IV. EVALUATION

The last step in the analysis of a public policy issue is to evaluate whether a public policy has had the desired effect: Has it worked? Since your paper will discuss a policy that has not been put into effect, an actual evaluation cannot be carried out. You can, however, indicate a plan for evaluating the effect of the policy.

To do this, begin by considering the problem you sought to remedy with the policy. Complete a list of the benefits and costs of the policy you advocated. Benefits are the advantages produced by implementing the policy. Costs include the direct expenditures required by the policy and the undesirable consequences that might result directly or indirectly from the policy. Once you have completed this list, discuss how each benefit and cost will be measured. The section must answer:

(1) What are the expected benefits of your proposed policy and how will you assess them?

(2) What are the expected costs of your proposed policy and how will you assess them?

You will find it difficult to measure benefits and costs because in some cases the expected results of a policy are intangible. However, with any public policy issue, even intangible benefits and costs can be measured through surveys of experts or groups affected by the policy. (Suggested length: 300 words)

Chapter 12

The New York Times As An Information Source

YOUR GOAL

To use the *New York Times* as a source in studying public policy issues by becoming familiar with its contents, identifying types of articles on public policy issues and knowing where to find information on public issues

---

Introduction

This chapter introduces *The New York Times* as a source of information in the study of public policy issues. One of the world's leading newspapers, it provides an excellent source of current information on public policy issues affecting the United States and the New York metropolitan area. It also provides some coverage of public policy issues affecting other states and local areas within the United States and many other countries. What makes *The New York Times* the newspaper of choice for introductory public policy analysis is the substantial background material and level of detail provided in its regular coverage. Another reason is that most political leaders view it as a source of information that will affect the evolution of public policy. (Guidelines provided in this chapter can also be applied to other newspapers.)

The in-depth study of public policy issues should begin with a study of past and recent articles of the newspaper. Back issues of the paper are available on microfilm.

Overall Content and Organization

If you become familiar with its content and organization, you can use *The New York Times* as a powerful tool for study of contemporary public policy issues. Here is how the editors of the newspaper suggest that you use The New York Times every day.

You don't read a newspaper the way you read a novel or a textbook or even a magazine. A paper like *The New York Times* is carefully organized so you can read it quickly. Headlines are written so you can get basic information even when time is very short.

First, they read all the headlines on page 1. Just the headlines alone give them a good idea of the major events of the day (the subheads give them even more information). Most people do this in less than a minute. Then, they read the news summary on page 2.

Next, they turn to the first page of the second section. It's called section B, Metropolitan News. Here is where readers find major stories about events and developments throughout the tri-state area, consisting of New York, New Jersey and Connecticut. For a quick idea of what's happening in the business world, they flip to the first page of Section D, Business Digest which gives them an idea of what they will be able to read later in that section. By following their example, for an investment of less than five minutes on this step, you will already know more than you could have found out anywhere else in twice the time.

The next step, which takes less than 10 minutes, is to go through the paper page-by-page, reading the headlines, looking at pictures, skimming an occasional article. People who do this don't usually have the time to read for details, but they learn a lot about what's going on in the world before they start their day, and they are far ahead of the game when they do.

If you follow a system like this for yourself, you'll probably come up with variations of your own to suit your own time schedule and range of interests. In general, *The New York Times* is organized in the same fashion every day. Understanding how it is organized helps you find your way to your special interests in less time.

It all begins with page 1, of course. It is where the editors put the "best" stories. What's meant by "best" could be the most important. It could also be the most unusual or most readable. The emphasis a newspaper places on any of these qualities determines the character of that newspaper.

The New York Times puts its first emphasis on the most important. But it does not neglect the other qualities at all. In fact, you will probably find all of them represented on a typical *Times* front page: articles that are not only important news, but also about unusual items and special interest stories. But since *The Times* believes its first duty is to inform, not just entertain, things you should know about always takes precedence.

You'll be able to know what the editors considered the most important story of the day because it will be placed to the top of the last column on the right. This may seem odd because we read from left to right. But the custom is related to two other customs. First, newspapers used to be arranged on newsstands folded with just the upper-right-hand corner showing. Second, *The Times* used to be arranged so that the lead story on page 1 continued from the bottom of that page to the top of page 2. Both of those old customs have changed, but the basic arrangement of *The Times'* front page has not.

The size of the headline over the top of the lead story is another clue to its importance. Occasionally, but not often, the headline extends across the top of the whole page. When it does, it's called a "banner headline."

The day's second-most important story appears at the top of the column at the extreme left. An exception to that rule is when the two most important stories are related to each other. Stories in similar fields are usually grouped together to help find your way to keep your own thinking organized.

Most page 1 stories "jump" or are continued on pages inside the paper. Here, too, the same kind of organization applies. A business news story would be continued in the Business Day Section. A story from Washington would be finished in the first section of the paper, Section A.

Related stories always appear together, and the news is arranged in general classifications. Foreign news appears on the first few pages of the first news section. It's followed in the same section by the national news report. Local news from New York, New Jersey, and Connecticut, follows in the Metropolitan News, Section B. And business news is found in Section D, Business Day.

Types of Articles on Public Policy Issues

Three types of articles can be found on public policy issues:

1. **News stories**--reports of events that constitute the societal conditions, the government actions, or activities of players concerning a specific public policy issue. (These terms are described in Chapter 1 of this book.)

2. **Background analysis**--articles that provide historical perspectives or specific information about societal conditions, players, or government actions. Sometimes these may accompany a specific news story. At other times, background analysis may be presented as a result of studies carried out by reporters or analysts.

3. **Opinion pieces**- -editorials prepared by the editorial board of the newspaper, letters to the Editor, or brief essays prepared by people who have a particular point of view. These articles appear on the two pages prior to the last page of Section A. They are called "opinion pieces" because when they cover public policy topics they express the views of the writer on the benefits or costs of existing policies and social conditions or on what government or non-government institutions should do about social conditions.

These types of articles frequently do not appear in pure form. Any given article may have elements of all three types. News stories will often have extensive background information and may report the opinions of players or experts on what policy should be followed. Background analysis can be found in the editorial pages and is frequently stimulated by news events.

Opinion pieces sometimes start with the description of a recent news event and are designed to provide background rather than express opinion on what should be done. However, for any given article, it is relatively easy to classify the article as primarily a news story, a background, or an opinion piece.

Where to Find Information on Public Issues

You will need to be able to locate news articles, background analysis, and opinion pieces relevant to public policy issues to complete much of the work in this book and to build an information base for public policy issues you wish to study "in depth." Of course, the editors and reporters of *The New York Times* do not announce at the beginning of an article that it is about a specific public policy issue. Rather they write about such things as new laws, which politicians are supporting what proposals, statistics on specific social conditions such as crime rate, unemployment and reading scores of high school students. They also report on specific events such as meetings of government officials, judicial decisions, or public statements.

Table: Types of Public Policy Issues	
Types	**Section of the Paper**
International-includes American foreign policy and major events and conditions in other countries.	First part of Section A.
US national	After first four pages in Section A and possibly beginning on first page if important.
New York metropolitan area includes city, suburbs, New Jersey, and Connecticut suburbs.	Section B unless major news event then begins on A.
Business and economic	Section D unless major event then begins on A.
Sports issues involving government policy.	Sports Sections daily and Section C on Mondays.
Science and technology questions as well as research background on any issue; also education issues.	Section C, Science Times published every Tuesday.

Articles from *The New York Times* should be used in completing Exercises in Chapters 1-10. For Chapters 5 through 10, you are expected to use additional sources as well, to become as knowledgeable as possible on your public policy issue. In order to do that, you will need to check on a systematic basis for stories relevant to your topic. Although, you may choose a topic that is not covered directly in *The New York Times*, you should still perform a quick search on every issue of the newspaper in case information on related topics is included.

CHAPTER 13

Editorials and Public Policy Analysis

YOUR GOAL

To identify, assess, and write the five types of public policy analysis found in editorials.

Introduction

A good analyst uses the following five types of analysis when discussing a public policy issue.

1. Monitoring societal conditions
2. Explaining societal conditions
3. Forecasting societal conditions
4. Evaluating societal conditions
5. Prescribing public policy

This chapter will help you to identify which types of public policy analysis are presented in editorials and op-ed articles.

MONITORING SOCIETAL CONDITIONS

Monitoring societal conditions is the process of observing and recording what is happening in society that gives rise to public policy issues. Like the biologist who carefully observes nature, the public policy analyst collects information about society.

Examples of Monitoring Societal Conditions

The federal debt increased from less than $1 trillion in 1990 to 2.2 trillion in 1987.

The New York State Office of Advocate for the Disabled information telephone referral service answered 11,988 calls in 1986, up 6% from 1985.

In 1980, there were an estimated 2.2 million homeless people.

Guidelines for Monitoring

1. **Present clear and precise information**. Look for a clear and specific description of societal conditions

2. **Give information that is as complete as possible**. Testing for completeness can be done by answering three questions:

A. Does the information provided allow for a comparison of conditions over time? It is better to know the number of traffic fatalities for each of the past five years than for only the most recent year.

B. Does the information make an effort to cover all parts of the society or does it deal with only certain areas or groups? In a study of New York State, reports on traffic fatalities only in New York City would not be adequate.

C. Does the information provide a basis for comparison between areas.

3. **Provide evidence that the information is accurate**. Cite books, articles, documents, or surveys used. Numbers and information provided without documentation cannot be trusted as much as those with documentation. Accuracy is always a problem in measuring social conditions, and the more known about how that information was collected the better.

EXPLAINING SOCIETAL CONDITIONS

Explaining societal conditions is describing what factors contribute to the conditions in society monitored in Step 14.1. If you have ever missed a curfew set by your parents, you may have attempted to explain why you were late. Explanation as a form of public policy analysis is similar, since it requires you to give the reasons why society is the way it is. The examples below provide several explanations of different societal conditions.

Examples of Explaining Societal Conditions

The Congress and administration are not willing to suffer the political consequences of cutting, spending, or raising taxes.

As disabled advocacy groups gain publicity, more people want to find out how to make use of their services.

Cuts in funding for food stamps, welfare benefits, and housing subsidies have made housing unaffordable for the poor.

Explaining why a condition exists is quite difficult because most societal conditions are caused by a large number of factors. For instance, the number of traffic fatalities in a particular area can be affected by the weather, the driving speed, and even the health of the economy. Research can give a general indication of which factors are important, but even the most elaborate studies fail to give absolutely complete explanations.

Guidelines for Good Explaining

1. *Cite as many relevant factors as possible*. Most societal conditions are caused by a large number of interacting factors. For example, juvenile delinquency may be caused by broken homes, peer pressure, low self-esteem, and several other factors. Therefore, single-factor explanations are almost always inaccurate. An attempt to consider a large number of factors is a sign that the analyst is trying to be as careful as possible in developing explanations. The following categories of factors should be considered: (1) economic, (2) geographic, (3) sociological, (4) political, and (5) psychological.

2. *Cite academic or government sources to support the factors you list*. For almost every public policy issue, studies exist that identify the causes of the conditions that have generated the issue. These studies are undertaken by scholars working in universities, research organizations, and also by government agencies. For example, in 1986, *The Final Report of the Attorney General's Commission on Pornography* contended that pornography is one of the factors responsible for a growing number of rapes and acts of violence against women.

   Chapter 4 will tell you how to locate these studies in the library. A good explanation will cite studies that demonstrate which factors contribute most to a social condition.

FORECASTING SOCIETAL CONDITIONS

Forecasting societal conditions is predicting what societal conditions will be like in the future. Like the weather forecaster who attempts to tell you in the middle of the week what the weekend weather will be, the public policy analyst makes forecasts about what society will look like several months, one year, or even ten years, down the road. Unfortunately, like the weather forecaster, uncertainty surrounds forecasts of social conditions. The farther into the future the prediction, the greater the uncertainty. The box below provides forecasts of several different societal conditions.

Examples of Forecasting Societal Conditions

The American federal debt will double within the next five years.

The number of calls to the Office of Advocate for the Disabled will increase by an average of 5% per month over the next year as more people find out about the referral service.

The number of homeless people will increase by 10% annually over the next three years.

Discussions of public policy issues are concerned with the future. All public policies are undertaken either to change future social conditions or to prevent changes. Forecasting, therefore, is critical to any public policy analyst.

Guidelines for Good Forecasting

1. ***Be clear with respect to what is being forecast and the time frame of the forecast.*** Forecasts are incomplete if they are unclear about the amount of increase, the time frame, and where the change will occur.

2. ***Cite academic or government authorities if possible.*** The best forecasts are backed up by government or academic studies and are made by individuals and groups who have expertise and have no vested interest in the conclusion of the forecast. A particularly useful approach is to find several forecasts by experts and to consider all their conclusions.

3. ***Make reasoning behind the forecast clear.*** If you are unable to find academic or government authorities to support your forecast, you will need to make clear your own reasoning for the forecast. Basically, you will make one of two types of forecast:

   A. Things will continue as they have been in the past. For example, "For each of the next five years, traffic fatalities in New York State will rise 5% per year" could be based on trends over the past decade which show a 5% a year increase.

   B. Things will be different from what they have been in the past. For example, "The number of traffic deaths in New York State will decline by 5% a year over the next five years because of increased use of seatbelts."

Both forecasts could be based on the same historical information over the past ten years. However, forecast B assumes that increased use of seatbelts will cause a change in the historical trend. Forecast A, on the other hand, assumes that increased seatbelt use will not make a major difference.

EVALUATING SOCIETAL CONDITIONS

Evaluating societal conditions is judging whether conditions in society are desirable or undesirable. A public policy analyst might conclude that the number of traffic fatalities is too high, or, if the trend is downward, that conditions are improving. Like teachers who grade your performance, public policy analysts determine whether society is performing up to levels they consider adequate.

Evaluation of societal conditions is important because the conclusion reached about whether there is too much crime, drug abuse, unemployment, or any other undesirable social condition, leads to decisions about whether new public policies are needed. The examples below provide several evaluations of societal conditions.

Examples of Evaluating Societal Conditions

The federal debt will unfairly burden future generations with staggering bills.

People who call the referral service benefit from being directed to the resource office that can best help them.

Too many homeless people die from exposure and lack of proper medical care.

Guidelines for Good Evaluating

1. *Be clear in identifying goals that should be used to judge social conditions.* Good public policy analysis requires a clear statement of what societal conditions are desired. For example, those supporting the mandatory seat belt law in New York State have the goal of fewer traffic fatalities. In many cases, the analyst takes for granted that the reader understands the importance of the goal of the analysis.

2. *Consider all major goals that are relevant to the public policy issue.* Most policy issues involve many goals, some consistent with one another, some in conflict. For example, a discussion of the mandatory seatbelt law can begin with the goal of preserving human life, but should identify other goals which may or may not be in conflict with saving lives. Some of these are (1) individual freedom, which many feel is reduced by the law; (2) the respect of government itself because of the difficulty in enforcing the law; (3) increased

costs to the taxpayers resulting from the enforcement costs: and (4) reduced car insurance premiums.

PRESCRIBING PUBLIC POLICY

Prescribing public policy is advocating what government action should be taken to promote good societal conditions. For example, the analyst might prescribe a mandatory seatbelt law, as the New York State government did in 1984, to reduce traffic fatalities. Like a medical doctor who prescribes an antibiotic to cure an infection, the public policy analyst prescribes a government action to reduce undesirable societal conditions or promote desirable ones. The examples below provide several explanations of different societal conditions.

Examples of Prescribing Public Policies

The federal government should double the gasoline tax.

The Office of Advocate for the Disabled should launch a publicity campaign to inform the public of the services they provide.

The amount of federal funds allocated to low-income housing program should be increased by 50%.

Guidelines for Good Prescribing

1. *Provide a clear prescription.* The analyst must be very clear about which policy is being recommended and at what level of government. Also, a goal must not be confused with a prescription.

2. *Provide several alternatives to the favored prescription.* While the analysis may clearly endorse a specific policy, it should also examine the alternatives. This will demonstrate that the analysis includes all the relevant factors. For example, if an analysis favors mandatory seatbelt legislation, it should discuss such alternatives as requiring air bags or spending more money on safety education.

3. *Assess the desirable and undesirable consequences of the prescription and the alternatives.* For each prescription suggested, the analyst should consider the good and bad consequences that might result directly or indirectly from the policy. Some attempt should be made to weigh the pluses and minuses for each policy and to reach a conclusion about why the favored prescription is preferred. For example, a mandatory seatbelt law may reduce traffic but it may have the undesirable consequence of limiting

individual freedom. An air bag law might reduce fatalities even more, but would be much more costly.

Chapter 14

Format For a Quantitative Research Paper

YOUR GOAL

To conduct and write a study using quantitative data.

Introduction

Decision-makers in government, business, and the non-profit world frequently need to acquire information in quantitative from. The reasons for this are discussed in Chapter 16. Sometimes the data is generated by surveys, which are discussed in Chapter 3 and Chapter 15, while sometimes the data comes from records or direct observations.

This chapter assumes that you are conducting research and writing a report for a public policy client under the supervision of an instructor. Its purpose is to guide you to complete your data collection and analysis efficiently. It also provides a specific format that will make your report as useful to the client as possible. If your client prefers a different format, you should adjust accordingly. However, the format presented in this chapter should be followed if the client does not indicate a preference or your instructor requires it.

The chapter begins with some suggestions on a variety of topics. It then moves on to the important question of planning and scheduling. The last section provides specific format guidelines that are very detailed.

General Guidelines

Experience is clearly the best teacher, but since you are probably undertaking this type of project for the first time, you have little experience upon which to build. Fortunately, we can learn from the mistakes of others. Students who have written reports and have learned the hard way provide the hints listed below. Take their lessons seriously.

Organizing Your Project

Selecting a Project

In selecting a project, use the following criteria:

- Your ability to complete all tasks required in the project
- Your interest in the subject with which the project is concerned
- Your ability to learn about the subject in order to complete the project
- Your ability to communicate with the prospective client
- Your ability to understand the objectives of the client
- Your ability to anticipate the technical pitfalls of the project
- Your ability to get to and from the client and other sites necessary to do your research
- Your access to a telephone for any necessary calls

The Work Done

Clients

- Get to know your agency
- Keep control of your client
- Be specific in your contract; don't let the client add tasks beyond what is initially agreed
- Learn the technical language of the client
- Do not pay for client's work such as phone calls or postage
- Do not be surprised if secretaries and others give you a hard time
- Maintain close contact with the client
- Do not take the client's behavior personally
- Call to confirm appointments within 24 hours of the agreed time
- Do not be misled by titles
- Make the client keep deadlines

132

- If the client is giving data or membership lists, acquire them immediately and check for quality. Don't believe in promises of lists or other information until you actually have your hands on them

Project

- Prioritize goals at the outset
- Do not underestimate the amount of time required
- Set firm, specific deadlines, and keep them
- Be specific with your client about the final product
- Do not rely on the client for most of the information
- Make sure that any information provided by the client is accurate and current
- Double check your data with the client before analysis
- Keep your paperwork organized
- Beware of sensitive information and keep it confidential
- Ask permission to quote
- Complete the final draft 48 hours before it is due
- Use your agenda as a planning and time management device

Surveying

- Subject knowledge is essential to good questions
- Pre-test your survey
- Make sure the target population is appropriate
- Anticipate delays in getting surveys back
- Get permission from the respondent to conduct the survey
- Make sure respondents' privacy and rights are respected

In General

- Complete a bibliography and talk to experts so you can learn as much as possible about the subject
- Be prepared for such serious computer problems as lost data files and unreadable disks
- Check with instructor early; keep notes
- Know your way around the area you're working in
- Do not be a spoiled brat
- Watch out for serious roadblocks; alert instructor at once

Planning and Scheduling Research Projects

This section is key to your success because poor plans and poor scheduling will lead to missed deadlines and a poor report. Follow the guidelines below.

In General

- You will have to provide your own transportation to and from the agency.

- Inquire about agency funds for any additional supplies required to complete the project.

- Keep all appointments with your agency contact.

- Your dress and conduct must, at all times, convey your position as a professional researcher carrying out an important project. Your behavior reflects upon you, and your program.

- Type your final report error-free and of presentation-quality which means setting sufficient time for proofing.

- Make three copies of your agency report. One copy is for your program's records, one will be sent to the agency, and one is for your files. It may be helpful to you in seeking an internship, a job, a scholarship, or admission to graduate school.

- Review past projects on file in the office to see what a good project looks like, and what has been done previously for your agency and related agencies.

- Maintain close contact with your instructor. Completing the project for this course is like completing a job. Your instructor is your boss. When you make an appointment, keep it or call the office at least 24 hours ahead of time to cancel and reschedule.

- Keep class time free of any other commitments, even when no formal class is held. Do not schedule client appointments at that time. Plan to contact the course professor during designated class times.

Agenda

The agenda is a critical self-management tool to make sure you have carefully planned the activities you need to undertake to complete a high quality project.   Discuss the agenda with your client as a way of communicating what you are planning to do and to see if the client has any comment on your plans.

The agenda will also be reviewed by the course professor to ensure that you are on track.   Carefully check the syllabus for the due dates of the agenda.

A sample agenda appears on the next page.   Note that this agenda is from a completed project.   You will need to save your first agenda and prepare a final one for your debriefing report.   Use a Microsoft Excel spreadsheet and use a format similar to the one on the next page.

Sally Student	Agenda through				12/1/96
PAF 315 Fall 1996					
Project: Effectiveness of ABC Organization					
Client: Jane Doe, ABC Organization of Central New York					
Item	Deadline	Date Done	Time Planned	Actual Time	Comment
1. First meeting with client	9/4	9/22	1	1	Overall plan for research determined
2. Diagnostic test, review spreadsheet commands	9/1	9/27	5	9	Had forgotten more than I realized
3. Second meeting with client	9/12	9/12	1	1	Questionnaire discussed and more planning
4. Telelphone calls with Jane	9/15	9/14	2	2	Confirmation of who will do what
5. Contract signed	9/6	9/6	1	2	Client out of town for 2 days
6. Preparation of spreadsheet programs	9/30	9/30	2	6	Programs had to be revised
7. Follow-up meeting with client	10/1	10/1	1	1	
9. Third meeting with client	10/7	10/7	2	2	Revise plans; collect questionnaires
10. Agency paper	10/10	10/10	4	6	Delay for printer to be repaired
11. Annotated bibliography	10/10	10/10	2	2	Library research completed
12. Call school for confirmation	10/10	10/13	1	1	Had to make several calls before making contact
13. Faculty report	10/11	10/14	4	6	Faculty not in office during scheduled hours
14. Collection of school surveys	10/11	10/11	1	1	118 questionnaires
15. Received pre-surveys from other schools	10/16	10/16	1	1	92 questionnaires
16. Received other post- surveys	10/23	10/23	1	1	83 questionnaires
17. Data input 25 cases	11/8	11/8	5	7	Pre-test at first school; entry didn't work right at first
18. Data input 25 cases	11/11	11/11	5	6	Pre-test at second school; had to wait for a computer
19. Update agenda	11/12	11/12	1	1	
20. Data input 50 cases	11/13	11/13	5	6	Post-test at first school
21. Data input the remainder of cases	11/13	11/13	5	4	Post-test at second school; f inally getting the hang of it!
22. Meeting with client	11/14	11/15	1	2	Client out of town on scheduled meeting day
23. Graph creations	11/15	11/15	5	3	Lots of false starts with charting program
24. Graph creations	11/16	11/18	10	12	Chart program not working as well as first time
25. First draft of Research Paper	11/22	11/23	3	4	Extra research needed
26. Revise draft	11/23	11/24	2	3	Reorganization needed
27. Make extra copies of Research Paper	11/23	11/23	1	1	
28. Draft Final Paper	11/24	11/24	1	2	More to it than I thought at first
29. Memo to Client	11/24	11/24	1	2	Kept thinking of extra things to say
30. Letter to faculty adviser	12/1	12/1	1	1	
Totals			75	96	

Format For The Report

Report Standards

- Produce a report that is camera-ready, double-space using a high quality printer. Do not use dot-matrix printers (even near letter quality), low quality typewriter ribbon, or erasable paper.

- Do not right-justify; instead, use a ragged-right margin.

- A cover sheet will be provided by the course instructor. Use this cover sheet or a clean copy of it for your title page.

- Paginate each page, beginning with the second page of text. Use a footer that summarizes the title with date. The footer should read: Title of Paper, Month, Year, Page Number (Senior Citizen Housing Needs Assessment, November 1999, Page 7).

- Bind the report by placing one large staple in the upper left-hand corner of the report.

- Make the report a self-contained document; do not refer to some print-out in the body of any paper.

- Place statistics associated with any figure immediately within, below, or beside the discussion, not on a separate page.

- Do not print in any color other than black and white, since other colors will not copy clearly. You may use shadings and hatch-marks in your graphs. Commentary must appear on the same page as the corresponding figure. Pay attention to how it will photocopy.

- Use simple, clear graphics.

- **Prepare a perfectly clean and properly formatted paper. No errors of spelling, style, or formatting are acceptable. Hand-made corrections are not acceptable.**

- **Each of the main sections of the report must be in all capitals and centered on the page. They are: EXECUTIVE SUMMARY, INTRODUCTION, METHODS, FINDINGS, ANNOTATED BIBLIOGRAPHY, AND APPENDIX 1-?**

Title Page

Begin the title 4" from the top of the page, centered between left and right sides. Type the title with a font similar to "Times New Roman" in all capitals, boldface, using a type size of 14-20, depending on the length of the title. Keep the title short and informative.

Avoid unnecessary words such as "study," "survey," and "report." In other words, do not produce titles such as "Report on a Survey Study of the Client Satisfaction with XYZ Agency." Instead, write "Client Satisfaction with XYZ Agency."

Starting 3" from the bottom of the page type a centered sub-title in boldface, using initial capitals and the same font, and about half the size of the main title, according to the following format:

A Study Conducted for the [Agency Client]
[Further identification of particular office, if appropriate]
by
[Your Name]
Month Year

See the sample title page on next page.

SENIOR CITIZEN HOUSING NEEDS ASSESSMENT

A Study Conducted for the Tully Housing Authority
by Jennifer Ayers
November 1999

Executive Summary

Write this section after the rest of the report is finished. Use your word processor to copy and paste from the rest of the report. Begin the Executive Summary on a new page. The title and the subtitle at the top of the executive summary page should follow the sample on the following page using bold-faced type. It consists of a title, the name of the agency, your name, and the date.

The executive summary consists of three paragraphs:
1. One paragraph summarizing the introduction to the report.
2. One paragraph summarizing the methods for gathering and analyzing data.
3. One paragraph summarizing substantive findings.

Boldface and underline the words Introduction, Methods and Findings. Use the same phrasing in the Executive Summary that appears in the body of the report.

Here are some general principles for your Executive Summary.

- Do not use the words 'I' or 'we.'
- The Executive Summary should be one page, but should fill up the entire page. You may use 10 instead of 12-point font size. (Use 12 for the rest of the paper.)
- Use past tense since you are reporting a study that has already been undertaken.

First Paragraph: Summarizing Introduction

- Good standard first sentences are: "This study reports information gathered through a survey conducted for _____. The study will assist _____ (the name of the agency) to _____.
- The first paragraph must always mention how the client will use the information.

Second Paragraph: Summarizing Methods

- Do not use 'approximately,' especially when referring to sample or findings.

- In the Methods paragraph, do not mention the questions or topics of the survey. These items will be discussed in the Findings section.
- Be specific about the target population and the sample. Give numbers of each. Be specific as to how a sample was chosen, and what percentage of the sample responded.
- Methods section should not contain findings except for the demographics of the respondents. In most cases, do not put the demographics, such as male-female distribution, in the Findings section unless the client requests it.
- Do not write in the Methods section that you tabulated the data or used a spreadsheet. This information is redundant and irrelevant (as is this sentence).

Third Paragraph: Summarizing Findings

- If possible, the findings should be listed in descending order of importance.
- The findings listed in the executive summary must be identical to the actual finding headlines in the Findings section of the report.

(*Sample Executive Summary*)

Senior Citizen Housing Needs Assessment
Tully Housing Authority
by Jennifer Ayers
November 1996

EXECUTIVE SUMMARY

Introduction: This study reports information gathered through a survey conducted for the Tully Housing Authority. The results will be included in a report to the United Way and the agency's Board of Directors. The report will be used to help assess the program and develop new policies.

Methods: The data for the study was generated through a telephone survey of individuals who have used the program over the past two years. Respondents were selected by choosing every third name from a master list of clients. From the target population of 304, a simple random sample of 100 was selected, and 74 responses were obtained. In the sample, 65% of the respondents were female, compared to 71% female in the target population.

Findings: Of the 74 respondents:

1. 82% received care from the Home Care Division for more than 6 months.

2. 57% learned about the agency from their doctor or hospital staff.

3. 80% of the patients indicated they received Very Good or Good services from the agency's home care nurses.

4. 86% of those receiving physical therapy found the services to be either Very Good or Good.

5. 78% of the patients have never had to reach agency staff members after hours or on weekends.

6. 92% of the patients have never had a problem reaching staff members.

Introduction

Provide background information about your project. Typical points which may be addressed include:

- Why the research was undertaken
- A definition of the problems being studied
- Any research discussion with client
- Previous research for which this is a follow-up
- A future larger project for which this is a pilot study
- What uses the agency will make of this report

(Not all of these points need be covered.)

The first sentence of your Executive Summary should be used as the first sentence of your introduction. Do not provide background information on your client or agency; they already know about themselves.

Methods

The purpose of the methods section is to explain to the reader, in as much organized detail as possible, the following:

- How you obtained the data
- How accurately the data represents what it is suppose to represent

These two topics apply regardless of the type of data you are using-- whether published information, information supplied by agency records, or surveys you are conducting yourself. Divide your Methods section using the two sub-headings below.

How Data Was Collected

In describing how you obtained the data, be as precise as possible. The test is this: Could the reader collect the data after reading your description? To ensure this, here are some guidelines:

- *For published sources*, provide full documentation and describe how the author of the source collected the data.

- *For information provided by the client*, describe the procedures used to obtain the data. Interview the client and others involved in collecting the information. Be sure to include all collection forms and to discuss how the data was recorded, and if relevant, include the final form you received.

- *For surveys*, you need to follow the guidelines in Chapters 3 and 15. Organize your discussion into the following categories:

  1. Instrument Design. Describe how the survey instrument (questionnaire) was designed and tested. Discuss who wrote it. Indicate if there was any pilot testing.
  2. Target Population and Sample. Define the target population and describe the sample selection process.
  3. Method of Contact. Procedures used to contact the respondents.

Quality of the Data

Discuss the quality of the data in terms of both its representativeness and its accuracy. Representativeness refers to whether the data provide a complete picture. If the data comprises all of the available information, then by definition it is representative. However, if it is a sample of the complete data, then you must discuss whether or not the sample reflects the total set of information. Accuracy refers to whether the data provided a "true picture of reality." Mistakes in recording information or deliberate misinformation or a lack of clarity about the data being collected detract from accuracy.

- *When using data from published sources:* You can comment on the reputation of the publisher or the author. A discussion of how vested interest might play a role is frequently required. The degree to which the source is cited by others and the history of the publication--how many previous editions--is also useful.

- *When using data from agency records:* Maintain a healthy skepticism since the agency is likely to argue that the data is accurate. Ask questions such as how many cases should you have and how many do you have. Frequently, an agency will claim that it has all of the records of its clients but when you look at the actual list, it is far fewer than the agency reports it has. Ask to look at the original documents. Look out for incomplete and illegible records. Ask how long the data has been collected and who is responsible for the data collection. Ask whether or not the information is sent to government agencies or funders.

- *When using survey data which you collect or is collected by the agency or someone else:* Assess the degree to which the sample is likely to reflect the target population by comparing distributions on key variables. Comment on whether or not the wording of the questions or the method of the contact may have introduced systematic bias or the respondent may have not provided an honest response.

Remember that there will always be questions about accuracy. Discuss them fully. If possible, provide suggestions on how to improve the accuracy of the data by improving data collection procedures. If appropriate, include revised forms and survey instruments in an appendix. The next pages contain an example of how the methods section should be organized for a survey.

METHODS

How Data was Collected

Instrument Design: The survey was created by the National Foundation for Consumer Credit. Because the Consumer Credit Counseling Service of Central New York had conducted similar survey studies, the national organization used their previous surveys as a guide in creating the new national standard survey. Therefore, the survey used could not be altered in any way because the national agency wanted to compare results between agencies throughout the United States. The researcher was not notified of any pilot testing of the final survey.

Target Population and Sample: The target population consists of 5,058 Consumer Credit Counseling clients from the committees of Syracuse, Ft. Drum, Utica, Binghamton, Colonie, Vestal, and Albany in New York State. The agency provided a sampling frame that included 1,277 clients. These clients were selected by printing the mailing labels of each counselor's clients at each location. Then, in an effort to represent each counselor equally, the first column of each counselor's label list was taken as the sampling frame. This represented a 25% random sample of the clientele at each location. A total of 394 responses were received out of 1,277 mailings (a 31% response rate).

Method of Contact: The questionnaires were mailed to the sample and mailed back to the agency. The agency then opened the responses to be sure that clients did not include their monthly payments in the envelopes. The agency also photocopied any questionnaires on which the clients reported problems that should be given immediate attention.

Quality of the Data

The sample population appears to be representative of the target population. The percentages received from each area closely match the percentages sent out to each area. There may be some error in this data because 131 out of the 394 respondents did not indicate on their questionnaire which area they were from. This figure represents 33% of the total number of questionnaires received. The design of the survey may have affected this statistic. The question on office location was not clearly stated or visible. When conducting next year's survey, the client should recommend to the national organization that the questionnaire be altered to make that item more easily seen. In any event, according to Figure 9, Chapter 16, these figures indicate no significant difference between population and sample.

Figure 14.1: Comparing Target Population to Sample (main sources of responses)			
	Target Population	Sample Indicating Their Location	Difference
Location	N=5058	N=263	
Syracuse	39%	39%	0
Utica	13%	11%	+2
Binghamton	18%	18%	0
Albany	30%	32%	-2

Those clients who included their name and detailed complaints about service were contacted by the agency to try to alleviate their problem as quickly as possible. This did not sacrifice the study's confidentiality statement because there was no space on the survey to place the respondent's name. When respondents did include their name, the agency took this as a request for immediate assistance. Because only 4% of the respondents provided their names and used the survey as a way to request action on their specific problems, this is not evidence of an overrepresentation of negative responses.

There were a total of 394 respondents in the survey. A small number of respondents left some of the questions blank. This explains why the frequencies are not the same for each graph. The sample size represents the number of people who actually answered a given question.

Findings

In this section, provide the agency with a brief summary of the conclusions of the study. Present findings as a series of short briefings that take the following form, in order, on a separate page for each finding:

- *Headline*: A brief statement summarizing a key point. The key point is usually the largest category (or group of categories) in a given finding. For example, if you find that 10% of respondents are "very satisfied" and 55% are "satisfied" with an agency, a headline could read: "65% of respondents are satisfied or very satisfied with the agency."

- *Figure*: A bar graph using the format in the sample graph on the next page properly labeled and numbered consecutively within the report. **Follow the formatting guidelines below:**

- Title the graph and label both axes
- Include "N =" under the title
- Use percentages, not raw numbers
- Include data labels
- Clear the background of the graph
- Do not code the category labels on the X-axis. For example, write "Male" or "Female," not "M"and "F."
- Identify the source for each graph

- *Comment*: Add a comment *only if necessary*. In most cases there will be no comments. Do not repeat the headline or summarize the findings presented in the figure. The purpose of a comment is to assist the reader in understanding the data presented in the figure by providing information that the reader may not have. Here are some of the primary types of comments you might make:

  - The data used is flawed by a poor sample or a poor question or missing responses.
  - A statistical analysis reveals that the pattern in the data presented is related to some other variable such as sex, age, location, or participation. This is a discussion of confounding variables. In some cases, you may want to put cross-tabulation tables in the comment or in the appendix to support your discussion.
  - The finding under discussion is related to a previous or subsequent finding.

If possible, list the findings in order of importance to the agency, starting with the most important. If that is not possible or appropriate, present the findings in some other logical order, such as the order in which the information was gathered (as from a questionnaire), or in order from the most surprising to least surprising.

For surveys and data sets with a large number of variables, you may want to group variables or responses into findings. If you wish to present a large number of results that do not warrant any comment, place them in an Appendix with a brief discussion in the Findings section.

Do not provide prescriptions, recommendations, or evaluations in the comments or anywhere else in the report.

See the sample finding presented in proper format below.

(Sample finding presented with a bar graph for a figure)

1. 74% of the agency's clients have used the agency's services for less than 100 hours during the past year.

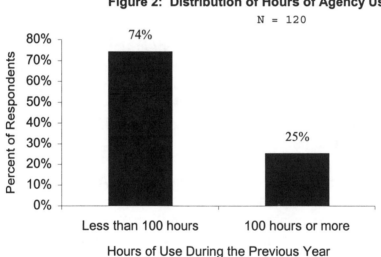

Figure 2: Distribution of Hours of Agency Use

Source: Data collected for the Tully Housing Authority by Jennifer Ayers, Research Project, Syracuse University, November 1999.

Comment: Many clients may not be aware of all the services available since many respondents were unaware that the Valley Service Office was actually a part of the agency's services. Consequently, these findings may under-represent the actual number of hours of agency use by clients.

Annotated Bibliography

Provide an annotated bibliography to help your client. The bibliography items most useful would be those that were attempts to carry out a study similar to yours. Other topics (listed in order of preference) that your client might find useful are on the types of programs being studied, evaluation or descriptions of the work of similar agencies, or generalized discussions of the causes of the societal problems your agency addresses.

To compile your bibliography, conduct a library search of books, articles, government documents and ask for leads from your client and your faculty advisor. Watch out for jargon-filled publications testing theory and containing little substantive information. These can usually be identified by an overuse of high level statistics, mathematics and obscure technical terms.

The annotated bibliography should appear immediately following the Findings Section and should open with a paragraph discussing the general availability and relevance of published material to the topic. It should then contain a citation and a brief discussion similar to the one below. Include as many as you consider useful to the reader. Do not include irrelevant items.

Prepare the annotated bibliography using the MLA Handbook style. Each entry must be followed by a brief *annotation*, a brief statement of how the item pertains to your project. On the next page is an example of a good entry. The topic of the student's project was providing assistance to child victims of sexual abuse.

Rothery, Michael, and Gary Cameron. *Child Treatment: Expanding Our Concept of Helping.* Hillsdate: Lawrence Erlbaum Associates, 1990. Issues dealing with child abuse discussed extensively in the last six chapters of the book. Topics emphasized include: treatment of abusers, family therapy, the coordination of programs, prevention, and self-esteem and depression. Provides examples of previous surveys and contained material useful in creating the questionnaire for the survey of agencies dealing with child abuse.

The annotation consists of one or more phrases, not complete sentences. It answers the questions: "Why is this item selected for the bibliography? How is it relevant to the project?"

Appendices

Clearly label and consecutively number the Appendices, using Roman numerals for each Appendix and Arabic page numbers for each section. For example, number page 1 of Appendix I as I-1; number page 6 of Appendix III as III-6. Appendices may contain copies of raw and untyped draft, samples, or similar material if it is appropriate and legible.

Include the following items in the Appendices if available. (All the items listed below are rarely included in one report):

- Blank questionnaire.
- Data frequencies listed on a copy of the questionnaire for each question rising procedure discussed at the end of the survey chapter.
- Individual responses to open-ended questions with similar answers grouped.
- CODEBOOK if a computer-readable data set is used. The codebook must follow a standard Excel format. (See next page for a sample codebook.)
- Computer printed listings of data if less than 5 pages.
- Technical information on the results of statistical analysis and documentary research.
- Sample of final product prepared as part of the project. For example, a cleaned listing or a revised questionnaire.

(Sample CODEBOOK)

Survey of Student Willingness to Volunteer, Citrus University, Fall 1999
Format: Excel 6.0

COLUMN	FIELD NAME	DEFINITION	FORMAT
A	ID	Student's identification number.	Value
B	LAST NAME	Student's last name.	Text
C	FIRST NAME	Student's first name.	Text
D	BIRTHDAY	Date of birth NA = Not available	Date
E	SEX	Sex of student	Text
F	TUTOR	Willing to volunteer for tutoring project? Y = Yes; N = No; NA = Not available	Text
G	CLEAN	Willing to volunteer for house cleaning project? Y = Yes; N = No; NA = Not available	Text Text

Chapter 15

Guide to Conducting Sample Surveys

YOUR GOAL

To design and implement a sample survey, and report your methods clearly.

Introduction

This chapter is a continuation of Chapter 3 where we introduced some basic concepts of survey research so that you could plan a survey. The purpose of this chapter is to provide more detailed steps in actually implementing the survey and providing some basic analysis of the results. The format for a comprehensive report of a survey study is described in the previous chapter.

The checklist below is a summary of Chapter 3 as well as the procedures on data collection and analysis provided in this chapter. Carefully, read the entire checklist before reviewing Chapter 3 and reading the rest of this chapter.

Check-List of Tasks Necessary for Conducting a Sample Survey

1. Determine what your client wants.
  1.1 Identify your client's goals.
  1.2 Indicate how each piece of information will help achieve the client's goals.
  1.3 Identify any others in addition to your client who will be able to use the information and how they will use it.

2. Identify your target population and how you will sample it.

2.1 Define precisely the target population that you will sample for your survey including location and size.

2.2 Indicate the size of the sample you plan to analyze, the approximate percentage this represents of the target population and the 95% confidence interval.

2.3 Indicate how you will select the actual individuals who will be in your sample.

2.4 Indicate at least one of the key variables you will use, such as gender or age, to compare the characteristics of the sample with the population. Indicate why you have chosen this as the comparison variable.

3. Create a plan for conducting the survey.

3.1 Indicate how you will contact the individuals to gather information (e.g., face-to-face, telephone, or mail). Justify your decision.

3.2 Estimate and justify an expected response rate. Indicate how many people you expect to contact to achieve your desired number of respondents.

3.3 Schedule the dates for conducting the survey.

4. Draft the questionnaire.

4.1 Write an introductory script or cover letter.

4.2 Write some questions to gather information with which to compare your sample to the target population.

4.3 Write the closed-choice questions and the response categories.

4.4 List any open-ended questions and indicate how you will record and report the answers.

4.5 Have the draft reviewed by your client, representatives of the population, and knowledgeable readers before you conduct the   pilot test.

5. Plan a pilot test of the survey.

5.1 Decide how many respondents you want for a pilot.

5.2 List what you expect to learn from the pilot.

5.3 Schedule when you will conduct and assess the pilot, and make any changes in the questionnaire.

5.4 Make needed changes in your questionnaire or approach to the respondent.

6. Plan data collection.

    6.1   Estimate the number of questionnaires and other materials you will need.

    6.2   Develop a detailed plan for administering questionnaires.

    6.2   Monitor data collection, testing your results against schedule and adjust procedures as necessary.

7.   Prepare a Summary of Frequencies

    7.1   Collect all of the questionnaires.

    7.2   Take a blank questionnaire and record with hash marks the responses of all the completed questionnaires.

    7.3   Use a spreadsheet program to tabulate your responses if it is quicker than doing it by hand.

    7.4   Take another blank questionnaire and write in the summary information.

If you have reviewed the checklist and if you have a draft of the survey using the guidelines provided in Chapter 3, you are ready to
(1) plan a pilot test; (2) plan your data collection; and (3) prepare a summary of frequencies.

TASK 1: PLAN A PILOT TEST

- Decide how many respondents you want for a pilot.
- List what you expect to learn from the pilot.
- Schedule when you will conduct the pilot.
- Make needed changes in your questionnaire or approach to the respondent.

Although you and your client may be pleased with the initial design of your questionnaire, it is important to test it on a small portion of the target population to ensure the clarity of questions and whether the information you collect is what your client wants. Pilot test your survey on a group of 5-10 members of the target population. Select members as representative as possible. For example, if the population consists of a 50-50 male to female ratio, select your pilot group to reflect the same proportion. However, do not focus too much energy on an exact match. It is important to pilot test your questionnaire quickly so that you can use the results to revise it, if necessary. After you have collected and tabulated the data from the pilot test, review each of the previous tasks to determine whether revisions are necessary.

You should pay attention to the design of the questions themselves, especially to the following two concerns:

1.Does the respondent understand the questions as intended? For example, when high school teachers were asked what the major problems they faced as a biology teacher were, the following choices were given:

___ poor test books   ___ lack of lab equipment
___ poor student preparation   ___ discipline

To the surprise of the surveyors, "discipline" was identified as the leading problem by more than 90% of the respondents. The surveyors were surprised because they used the word "discipline" to mean the "discipline of biology," whereas the teachers saw it as coping with unruly student behavior.

2. Is the information generated by the question what the client wanted? For example, a question asked during a pilot test for the evaluation of the Teens Teaching Spanish program was:

Would you continue in this program if you had more time? ___ *Yes* ___ *No* ___ *Not Sure*

75% of the respondents answered "No," whereas 95% answered on a previous question that they had learned a lot from the program, and that they had enjoyed it. We found out that most of them answered "No" because they felt that they had learned as much Spanish as they thought they needed. The surveyors intended the question to determine whether the participants had a positive attitude about the program. Therefore they added, "*If 'No' why not?*" to the question to see whether or not the "No" answer measured negative attitudes.

TASK 2: PLAN DATA COLLECTION

- Estimate the number of questionnaires and other materials you will need.
- Develop a detailed plan for administering questionnaires.
- Monitor data collection testing your results against schedule and adjust procedures as necessary.

156

These tasks require serious attention to detail and appreciation of the power of Murphy's Law: "What Can Go Wrong, Will Go Wrong." Check to make sure that the required number of questionnaires is produced on time. A mistake that sometimes occurs is that the pages for a multi-page questionnaire are collated in the wrong order. Do not assume those who are administering the questionnaire will be as concerned about meeting deadlines and collecting responses as you are. Maintain a checklist that requires you to double-check with those responsible for distributing and collecting or mailing and receiving the questionnaires. Establish target dates when you expect to have 25%, 50%, 75%, and 100% of the questionnaires returned. Remember the 80-20 rule: in this case, it means that you will receive 80% of the questionnaires within the first 20% of the time allocated while the last 20% will be received very slowly. Determine a realistic cut-off date and don't accept any questionnaires after that date unless your response rate is far below what you expected. For telephone surveys, start early. Try a variety of days of the week and times of the day, and be ready for many disconnected telephones and quick hang-ups. Don't call too late, too early, or at dinner-time. If a respondent is not available, or you reach an answering machine, attempt to contact them at least two more times.

TASK 3: PREPARE A SUMMARY OF FREQUENCIES

- Collect all of the questionnaires
- Take a blank questionnaire and record with hash marks the responses of all the completed questionnaires.
- Take another blank questionnaire and write in the summary information.
- Use a spreadsheet program to tabulate your responses if it is quicker than doing it by hand.

Although you will probably want to prepare a formal report on the findings of your survey, you will always need to do a preliminary analysis of the frequencies of responses to each question. The format shown in this section is easy to prepare and can be used to show your client the initial results. This preliminary analysis will help you to decide what kinds of graphs and tables as well as statistics you might want to use.

To illustrate, let's assume that you have asked 50 people to answer the following as part of a questionnaire:

1. What is your gender? ___ Male ___ Female

2.Did you wear a seat belt the last time they drove a car?
__ Yes __ No __ Don't Know

3.Briefly describe what you do when a passenger in a car you are
driving refuses to wear a seat belt.

After collecting the 50 completed questionnaires, take a blank questionnaire on which to record the information. After five questionnaires, the one on which you were recording might look like this:

1.What is your gender? _///_ Male _//_ Female

2.Did you wear a seat belt the last time they drove a car?
_//_ Yes _//_ No _/_ Don't Know

3.Briefly describe what you do when a passenger in a car you are
driving refuses to wear a seat belt.
- Nothing (2)
- No Answer (2)
- Don't start until they buckle up (1)

Once your recording was done, you would copy the results on another blank questionnaire, resulting in something like this:

1.What is your gender? (28) Male (22) Female

2.Did you wear a seat belt the last time they drove a car?
(35) Yes (10) No (5) Don't Know

3.Briefly describe what you do when a passenger in a car you are
driving refuses to use a seat belt.
- Nothing (21)
- Give reasons why important (12)
- Don't start until they buckle up (9)
- No answer (8)

If you have only a few questionnaires to analyze, you can do your tabulations by hand. For larger surveys, you should use a spreadsheet or database program to tabulate the responses. When tabulating by hand, follow the steps above.

Chapter 16

Quantitative Skills

YOUR GOAL

To explore basic quantitative analyis tools in policy research.

Introduction

In this chapter you will be introduced to the skills necessary to interpret conditions relevant to public policy using statistical analysis.

The making and analyzing of policy are increasingly dependent upon the use of numbers and graphs. We use numbers in almost every aspect of communication. Our favorite sports team is described as "Number 1." Academic performance is described by the Grade Point Average (GPA).

Numbers and graphs can convey an idea in a form that is both interesting and clear. Once you learn the basics of presentation, you will find that with numbers and graphs, you can make an argument more effectively than with words alone.

People collect and interpret numerical data when they analyze public policy issues for two primary reasons:

1. Numbers are helpful in acquiring a general grasp of factors affecting public policy issues.

2. Numbers can provide a precise statement about those factors. Only by the use of numbers can precise comparisons be made between different locations, periods of time, and target populations.

| Statement 1: | This year's unemployment is worse than last year's unemployment. |
| Statement 2: | Unemployment in New York State is 6.2% this year, compared to 5.5% last year. |

Consider the two statements in the box above. The second statement is preferable to the first statement because it communicates both a general picture of social conditions and a precise measure. It indicates that unemployment is higher this year than last and by how much. It also indicates the geographical area to which the statement applies.

Numbers and graphs can be used in all areas of public policy analysis, but they are most extensively used to measure societal conditions. Figure 1 presents examples of data that might be found in each of the three components of public policy issues described in Chapter 1.

Figure 1: **Examples of numerical data used to describe the components of public policy issues**

Societal Conditions	Players	Public Policies
Unemployment	Survey of attitudes of	Government expenditures
Inflation	legislators	
Economic growth	Political contributions received	Tax rates
Tax payments		
Traffic fatalities	Legislative voting records	Minimum wage
Drug use		
	Patterns of party	Social security
School attendance	representation	benefits

The use of numbers and graphs in public policy analysis requires the completion of three tasks:

1. Selecting the most appropriate numerical information available.

2. Selecting the most appropriate type of analysis and display.

3. Making an interpretation that relates the analysis and display to the public policy.

Interpreting numerical information means explaining the reasons behind the information and drawing an inference about the information. More specifically, interpretation means providing the following:

- Summarizing the main point of what the numbers say, frequently presented as a headline above the table or graph.

- Explaining the reasons for the conditions shown by the numbers.

- Drawing conclusions from the numbers. Depending on your purpose, any conclusion may take one or more of several forms: Evidence for the existence and magnitude of a societal problem; an underlying factor contributing to the existence of a societal problem; an evaluation of the effects of previous policies on a societal problem; or the history and forecast of a societal problem for which you are proposing a policy solution.

The rest of this chapter describes and illustrates some additional principles of using tables and graphs in analyzing policy. It covers the following topics:

1. Scaling numbers

2. Presenting data with tables

3. Presenting data with bar graphs

4. Using trend lines

5. Displaying components with pie charts

6. Describing differences with percentages

7. Comparing two groups

1. Scaling Numbers

Whenever you use numbers in a table or graph, report them in such a way that they are easy to compare and interpret. It is usually better to report comparable numbers, such as percentages, or per capita rates rather than raw numbers. Making the numbers comparable is called scaling.

In many cases, converting raw numbers to percentages is enough to make them easy to interpret. For example, suppose 2,514 employees work in a state environmental agency. Of these employees, 274 are assigned to enforcement of illegal toxic dumping. The percentage of those assigned to enforcement is:

$$\frac{274}{2,514} \quad = \quad .10899 \text{ (rounded)} \quad * \quad 100 \quad = \quad 10.9\%$$

A percentage is one form of a "rate," which means the number of things per some other number, a commonly used rate is 100, 1,000, or some other multiple of 10. A percentage is a rate per 100. Another example of a rate is infant mortality, which is calculated as the number of infant deaths per 1,000 live births.

Another form of a rate is the difference between raw numbers and those reported in a more appropriate scale. The following table shows the number of traffic deaths in a selected group of states:

Figure 2: Total traffic deaths in selected states, 1985

State	Deaths
California	4,999
New York	2,065
Alabama	939
Massachusetts	663
New Mexico	497

Source: National Safety Council. The World Almanac and Book of Facts. New York: Newspaper Enterprise Association, 1986. p. 781.

Does this mean that California and New York are the most dangerous places to drive, while Alabama, Massachusetts, and New Mexico are the safest? Not necessarily. Part of the reason that California and New York have many traffic deaths, and that Alabama,

Massachusetts and New Mexico have few traffic deaths, may be the difference in the number of miles driven in each state. It is better to report the traffic death rate, that is, the number of deaths divided by the number of miles driven in each state. The usual method of reporting automobile traffic death rate is the number of deaths for each 100 million miles driven. Since very high numbers of miles are driven in California and New York, their high traffic death totals are divided by large numbers, which tends to lower their death rate. On the other hand, Alabama and New Mexico have fewer drivers and fewer roads, so their traffic death totals are divided by a smaller number, making their death rate higher. What about Massachusetts? It has a fairly low death total; it also has a high number of miles driven. Where will it rank when its traffic death total is divided by the miles driven in the state?

The answer is given in the following table, where the states are listed according to their traffic death rate -- total traffic deaths per 100 million miles driven:

Figure 3: **Traffic death rate per 100 million miles driven, selected states, 1985**

State	Deaths per 100 Million Miles Driven
New Mexico	4.3
Alabama	3.1
California	2.9
New York	2.4
Massachusetts	1.7

Source: National Safety Council. The World Almanac and Book of Facts. New York: Newspaper Enterprise Association, 1986. p. 781.

In the table above, the rankings are quite different. New Mexico and Alabama have the highest death rates, California and New York are in the middle, and Massachusetts has the lowest traffic death rate.

The scale you use depends on the kind of information you are reporting. Often percentages are used, which means that each number is divided by the same total. This shows what fraction each number represents of the entire total. Examples of such presentations include

163

budget figures, racial composition of a city, and the number of males and females in particular occupational groups.

Another common way of presenting numbers is on a per capita basis, in which each number is divided by the population of the unit (for example, school, city, or state) being reported. Examples include crime rates in different neighborhoods of a city, and income levels in different cities. Sometimes, if numbers involved are quite small, the figure is reported not in terms of the number of people, but in terms of 100 or 1,000 people. Some commonly used figures are reported as percentages, such as unemployment rates, which means the number of unemployed individuals per 100 people in the labor force looking for work.

To convert raw numbers to numbers that can be easily compared, do the following:

1. Decide if the raw number is adequate without making some conversion. This is possible in some rare instances. If not, go to step 2.

    For the example of traffic deaths, the raw numbers for traffic deaths are shown below.

California	4,999
Alabama	939
New York	2,065
New Mexico	497
Massachusetts	663

2. Choose the unit that should be divided into the raw number to allow for comparisons. As noted above, you may want to use the total which would give you a percentage or per capita figure.

    For the example of traffic deaths the unit chosen, 100 million miles travelled, is shown below.

California	1,724
Alabama	303
New York	860
New Mexico	116
Massachusetts	390

164

3. Divide the raw number by the unit number. Clearly label the number and provide a specific description of the source.

For the example on traffic deaths, the division and scaled numbers, total traffic deaths per 100 million miles travelled, are shown below.

California	$\dfrac{4,999}{1,724}$	=	2.9
Alabama	$\dfrac{939}{303}$	=	3.1
New York	$\dfrac{2,065}{860}$	=	2.4
New Mexico	$\dfrac{497}{116}$	=	4.3
Massachusetts	$\dfrac{663}{390}$	=	1.7

Source: National Safety Council. The World Almanac and Book of Facts. New York: Newspaper Enterprise Association, 1986. p. 781.

2. Presenting Data with Tables

Data must be presented in a form that is both interesting and clear. Stringing numbers together in a text does not accomplish either of these goals. For example, consider the following hypothetical example:

> A recent study, "Committee for the Aging: Research and Education" (CARE) indicates that, in 1920, the percentage of the United States population 60 years of age and over was 6%; in 1940, the percentage was 8%; in 1960, it was 13%; in 1980, it was 15%; and in 2000, it is forecast to be 20%.

Such information is difficult to understand presented in this way. If arranged in a table, as below, it is much easier to read. Note the "f" at the end of the year 2000, indicates the figure for that year is a forecast.

Figure 4: From 1920-2000 the percent of the United States population at least 60 years of age, is expected to grow to one-fifth of the total population.

Year	Percentage
1920	6%
1940	8%
1960	13%
1980	15%
2000f	20%

Source: "Committee for the Aging: Research and Education." New York: CARE, 1985.

Tables are a widely used and accepted means of organizing small sets of data for rapid visualization and understanding. A table requires:

- A title which clearly explains its nature or indicates its main point.

- Data elements carefully listed in some logical order (by time, in rank order, or some other sequence) under headings which clearly specify units of measurement.

- Documentation of the data source. Indicate the title of the source and a complete bibliographical reference, as described in Chapter 2. Just listing the organization issuing the information is not adequate. If the source is a newspaper, cite the title of the story, date, and page number. For a list of citation forms, see page 12.

3. Presenting Data with Bar Graphs

An even more striking way of presenting data is to use a bar graph, which is a series of parallel bars (or similar markings) placed either vertically or horizontally to indicate totals or percentages. In the construction of a bar graph, the length of the bars and the space between them should be consistent and allow for clear visual inspection. Normally a vertical (or y) axis is drawn with the scale placed alongside, while the horizontal (or x) axis is labeled with what units are being compared or measured. Bar graphs should be used any time you want to compare two or more units (for example: states, cities, years, or sub-groups of a population).

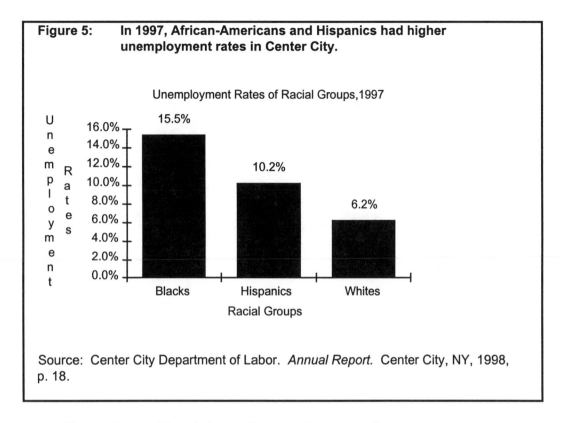

Figure 5: In 1997, African-Americans and Hispanics had higher unemployment rates in Center City.

Unemployment Rates of Racial Groups, 1997

Source: Center City Department of Labor. *Annual Report.* Center City, NY, 1998, p. 18.

Figure 5 provides information on the rate of unemployment among different segments of the population for the first quarter of 1997 in a hypothetical city. Each bar represents a different segment of the employable population, with the actual rate printed at the top of the bar. The height of the bars allows the reader to see the difference in unemployment of different racial groups.

4. Using Trend Lines

A trend line is a common form of graph. The trend line is derived from plotting time in years, months, or days on the x-axis (horizontal), and plotting the factor which is changing over time on the y-axis (vertical). This type of graph shows the progress of that which is on the y-axis over time. The trend can also be projected into the future. In the figure below, the forecast data is represented by a different symbol. This type of display is useful in monitoring and forecasting social conditions. Figure 6 shows the trend from 1990 projected through 2000 on the number of deaths expected from AIDS in a hypothetical city.

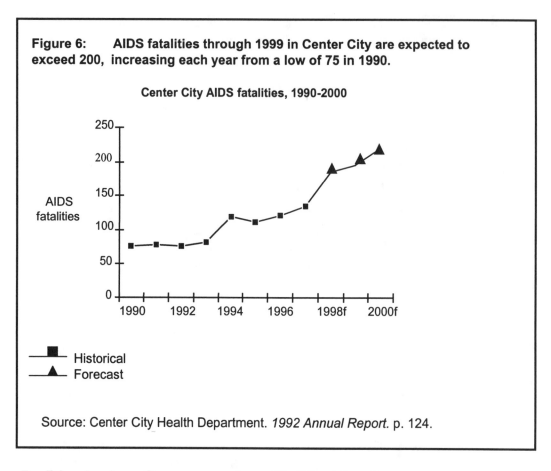

Figure 6: AIDS fatalities through 1999 in Center City are expected to exceed 200, increasing each year from a low of 75 in 1990.

Center City AIDS fatalities, 1990-2000

AIDS fatalities

■ Historical
▲ Forecast

Source: Center City Health Department. *1992 Annual Report.* p. 124.

5. Displaying Components with Pie Charts

A pie chart can be used to show how the component parts of a total are divided. The distribution of government spending or the ethnic composition of a political party are examples of subjects that can be displayed using this technique. To construct a pie chart, remember that the total of 100% is described by a circle of 360 degrees. Thus, each percentage point is equal to an arc of 3.6 degrees. To illustrate, we will construct a pie chart to show the distribution of people over 60 years of age in a hypothetical city as outlined in Figure 7. Each percent figure in the table below is multiplied by 3.6 degrees to determine the size of the arc that must be drawn for each segment of the pie.

Figure 7:	Age distribution of residents age 60 and above				
Age Group	**Percent**				**Arc (degrees)**
60 - 64 years	29.7	x	3.6	=	106.92
65 - 74	43.6	x	3.6	=	156.96
75 - 84	21.1	x	3.6	=	75.96
85 and older	5.6	x	3.6	=	20.16
Total	100.00%				360.00

If necessary, use a protractor to measure the necessary degrees on the circle. Each segment should be labeled with both a name and a percent. Labels may go either inside or outside the circle. Labels should be placed outside if the sections are especially narrow. As illustrated in Figure 8, the pie chart can be an effective technique for the visual display of data. They are not, however, appropriate for all displays. Pie charts containing more than eight segments, or containing several segments with very small arcs (less than 5%), are difficult to label and interpret.

Figure 8: **About one-fourth of Center City's residents over age 60 are among the "Very Old" -- 75 years and older.**

Age Distribution of Residents Age 60 and Above

Center City, 1992

85 and Older
6%

75-84
21%

60-64
Years
30%

65-74
44%

- ■ 60-64 Years
- □ 65 - 74
- ▨ 75 - 84
- ▦ 85 and older

Source: Committee for the Aging: Research and Education. The Needs of the Very Elderly. Center City, 1992. p. 5.

6. Describing Differences with Percentages

A percentage difference is a simple, but powerful tool for comparing two sets of numbers. You may want to determine the differences between estimated and actual budget figures, or between one year's crime rate and another's. Percentages are used to determine precise differences in three ways:

1. Comparison of estimated to actual. For example, the original estimate of the Federal budget deficit for 1983 was $113.65 billion, but the actual deficit was $195.4 billion. The actual figure was 73% higher than the estimate.

2. Comparison between numbers for the same period of time For example, in 1986, the population of the U.S.S.R. was 279.5 million and the population of the U.S. was 241.6 million. The population in the U.S.S.R. was 15.7% larger than the U.S. population.

3. Comparison between two periods of time For example, the number of felonies in New York City was 637,451 in 1981, while the number fell to 538,051 in 1984. The difference between 1981 and 1984 was a 16% decline.

Here is the procedure for calculating percent differences:

$$\frac{\text{New Figure - Original Figure}}{\text{Original Figure}} \quad * \quad 100 \quad = \quad \text{Percent Difference}$$

For example (from point 3, above):

$$\frac{\text{1984 Felonies - 1981 Felonies}}{\text{1981 Felonies}} \quad * \quad 100 \quad = \quad \text{Percent Difference}$$

$$\frac{538,051 - 637,451}{637,451} \quad = \quad \frac{-99,400}{637,451} \quad = \quad -.1559 = \quad -16\%$$

If you are comparing two numbers in the same time period, you may use either one as the "new figure," and the other as the "original figure."

One question you must answer when comparing percentages is "How big is big enough to make a difference?" Suppose, for example, you conduct a survey of two different high schools to find how many seniors are planning to attend college. Suppose in one school 87% plan to go to college, and in the other school 88% plan to attend college. With numbers so close, it would not make sense to conclude that the two schools differ significantly regarding college attendance. But what if the two figures were 87% and 89%? Or 87% and 92%? Or 87% and 97%? At what point would you be justified in saying the two schools were significantly different?

Fortunately, statisticians have developed a systematic procedure for making such conclusions. It is based on how many individuals are in each of the two groups being compared, as well as the magnitude of the percent difference between the two groups. This procedure is summarized in Figure 9 on the next page. To use the table, find the size of one of your groups (either one) somewhere down the row of the table. If the group size is between numbers on the row of the table, use the smaller number. Then find the appropriate column based on the size of the other group (again, using the smaller number if the actual group size is between numbers shown on the columns). At the intersection of the row corresponding to the size of the first group and the column corresponding to the size of the second group is a number. That number tells you how big the percentages between two groups must be before concluding that there is a significant difference. The table is based on a confidence interval of 95%. In other words, the table will give correct results in 95 out of 100 cases.

To illustrate how to use the table, consider the sample of the two schools mentioned above. The table tells us that a difference of one or two percentage points (87% to 88%, or 87% to 89%, for example) would not be significant even if the size of the groups surveyed in the two schools consisted of 3,000 students each. Even with such huge groups a difference of at least 3 percentage points would be required to conclude that a significant difference existed. The table also shows that even a difference of 10 percentage points (87% to 97%, for example) should not be considered significant unless one of the groups consisted of at least 150 students and the other group consisted of at least 300 students. From this table you can see why it is important to obtain large samples. Unless you have samples of well more than 100, you must obtain huge differences in percentage points to conclude difference between groups. If the size of either or both of your groups does not exactly match the table, use the next smaller figure on the table. This is a conservative decision, which you should always follow in statistical procedures.

171

Figure 9: Minimum difference in percentage points required to conclude that there is a statistically significant difference between two groups of different sizes (with 95% confidence).

One Group is at Least	The Other Group is at Least:									
	30	50	90	150	300	600	1000	1500	2000	3000
30	25	23	21	20	19	19	19	19	19	18
50	23	20	18	16	15	15	15	15	15	14
90	21	18	15	14	12	12	11	11	11	11
150	20	16	14	12	10	9	9	9	9	9
300	19	15	12	10	8	7	7	7	7	6
600	19	15	12	9	7	6	6	5	5	5
1000	19	15	11	9	7	6	5	4	4	4
1500	19	15	11	9	7	5	4	4	4	4
2000	19	15	11	9	7	5	4	4	4	3
3000	18	14	11	9	6	5	4	4	3	3

7. Comparing Two Groups

Many times in analyzing societal conditions it is important to see how two groups can be compared with one another with respect to an opinion, behavior, or how they have been affected by previous policies. Here, for example, are some questions that policy analysts may want answered:

- How do athletes and non-athletes in a high school differ with respect to a proposed "No pass, no play" policy concerning athletic eligibility?

- How do parents and students in a survey differ with respect to support for a proposed environmental policy?

- How do two different cities differ with respect to their crime rates?

A properly constructed table can help provide answers to these questions. Such a table is a cross-tabulation of two different variables.

For example, consider the first question above, how athletes and non-athletes differ with respect to a proposed "No pass, no play" policy. Assume that a survey has been conducted at a high school, that the sample was randomly selected according to the guidelines in Chapters 3 and 15, and that the sample contains both athletes and non-athletes. Suppose that one of the survey questions was:

"What is your attitude regarding the proposed rule under which any school athlete who is not passing in all courses will be ineligible to compete for the school: ___AGREE ___DISAGREE"

Further assume that of 300 students surveyed, 90 were athletes and 210 were non-athletes. Of the 90 athletes, 30 agreed with the policy and 60 disagreed. Of the 210 non-athletes, 160 students agreed with the policy, and 50 disagreed.

These results can be clearly shown in a table as follows, in which the two different groups (athletes vs. non-athletes) are used to form the vertical columns, and the answers are shown in the horizontal rows.

Figure 10: Athletes and non-athletes differ significantly regarding the proposed "No Pass, No Play" policy.

Attitude Toward "No Pass, No Play"	Type of Student		
	Athlete	Non-Athlete	TOTAL
Agree	30	160	190
	(33%)	(76%)	(63%)
Disagree	60	50	110
	(67%)	(24%)	(36%)
TOTAL	90	210	300
	(30%)	(70%)	

(Percentages may not add to 100% because of rounding)

Source: Student Survey, Central High School, Fall semester.

This table conveys a great deal of information when used with the appropriate tables and statistics.

1. The marginal totals and percentages to the right indicate the overall support for the proposed policy: 63% agree and 36% disagree. Note that 63% + 36% does not add to exactly 100% because of rounding. It is quite common, and no cause for concern, to have rounded percentages that should add to 100% actually add to 99% or 101%.

2. The marginal totals and percentages along the bottom row indicate the distribution of the sample: 70% non-athletes and 30% athletes. This figure might be used to check the representatives of the sample. Since Figure 1 (p. 30) tells us that a sample of 300 should have a target population of between 24% and 36% athletes (30% +/- 6%), we could check school records to see if the number of athletes was actually within that range. If the percentage of athletes was within that range, this would be evidence that our sampling procedure gave us a representative sample. If it turned out that there were fewer than 24% athletes or more than 36%, this would be a warning that our sampling was not actually as representative as we thought, that we had somehow introduced bias into the sampling process.

3. The column percentages comparing the agreement and disagreement of the two groups make clear how sharply the athletes and non-athletes differ on the question of the policy. As Figure 9 (p. 172) shows, when you have one group of 30 (the number of athletes who agree with the policy) and another group of 90 (the number of non-athletes who agree), a difference of at least 21 percentage points is required to be 95% confident that there is a statistically significant difference between the two groups. The difference in the table is 43 percentage points (76--the percentage of non-athletes agreeing, minus 33 --the percentage of athletes agreeing.) Since the 43 percentage points are much higher than the 21 point minimum in the table, we can say, with 95% confidence, that athletes and non-athletes clearly differ on the policy.

In other cases, the figures you present may be averages or rates rather than percentages. For example, you might compare crime rates in two different communities, or average tax rates in two different school districts. The principle is the same, using the groups to define the columns, and presenting comparable numbers in each row.

Examining the side-by-side column percentages is a quick way to compare groups, especially when they are of different sizes. This is why it is necessary to present not just totals, but also percentages or other comparable figures. Statistical procedures, which are not covered in this chapter, exist for determining when figures other than percentages are large enough to conclude that the two groups are significantly different. For this reason, it is preferable to convert numbers to percentages, and then use the table of minimum required percentage point differences.

Chapter 17

Research Designs for Evaluating Social Programs

*This chapter is an adaptation of the learning package titled, "Designs For Evaluating Social Programs, " by Lawrence P. Clark published in 1976.

YOUR GOAL

To choose an appropriate research design to evaluate a public policy or program.

Introduction

This chapter introduces you to ways of evaluating the impact of social programs on society. Such programs can range in scope and subject matter from a federal program to support preschool education for children from poor families to actions undertaken by a police department in a small town to curtail vandalism. This chapter will help you come up with an approach to collecting and analyzing data that provide as good a basis as possible to determine the impact of such programs.

Given the growing complexity of our society and the need for collective action not only by government, but also by groups with public responsibilities (e.g., the United Way), it is difficult to determine the impact of a given program. It is desirable to conduct rough estimates of whether a program is working or not because unsystematic observation and informal judgements fail to take into account factors that might be operating with respect to a given program. For that reason, it is necessary to develop research designs, which generate information that reflects as systematic a view of the impact of a program as possible.

This chapter is divided into three parts:

1. The Need for Research Design

2. Basic Concepts Necessary to Understand Types of Research Designs

3. Pre-Experimental Designs

Each of these sections introduces the basic ideas through a brief explanation and Part 1 includes an exercise in which you apply the idea to a specific example.

Given the complicated nature of the world and the difficulties associated with collecting data the most frequently used designs are pre-experimental. In a few cases, quasi-experimental are used. The discussion of true experimental designs is not included because they are never used in serious policy discussions of social or economic conditions.

PART 1: THE NEED FOR RESEARCH DESIGN

To understand why it is necessary to evaluate any given social program with a systematic plan to collect and evaluate data, consider the following example.

Suppose that you feel ill on Monday, visited the health service on Tuesday and received a one-day supply of pills to alleviate the problem. On Wednesday you feel fine.

The physician then asks you whether you feel better. You tell him, "Yes," truthfully. Assume for simplicity that, in fact, your health status has improved.

Based on this simple comparison of your condition before receiving the pill versus after, the physician infers that the pill has "worked," i.e., that the treatment's effects were positive. The size of the effect is gauged from the size of the improvement in health status from the following graph:

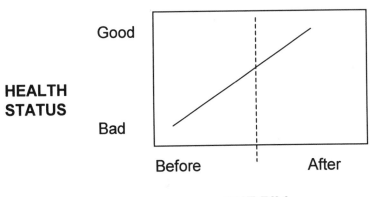

HEALTH STATUS

Good

Bad

Before | After

THE PILL

The steeper the slope from A to B, the greater the improvement in health status.

The information portrayed on the graph appears to indicate that the medicine worked. However, it is possible to think of a variety of other explanations for your recovery that had little or nothing to do with the medicine. Listed below are many plausible alternative explanations.

1. Your body's natural defenses may have taken care of whatever was causing your illness.

2. Your health status might have changed because you pulled an all-nighter studying for an exam.

3. Your health status might have changed because of an interaction between the pill and some other drug you were taking.

4. You may have decided that on second thought, you weren't really sick after all on Monday.

5. You might feel better because going to the doctor gave you a sympathetic person to tell your troubles to.

6. Your health status might have changed just by going to see a doctor in his office.

7. You might be feeling better because Wednesday, unlike Monday, is a bright, sunny day.

These plausible alternative explanations fall into various categories that will be discussed in detail in Part 3. The point of the discussion here is to demonstrate that the casual observation of the impact of any action on anything leaves a great deal to be desired, particularly when people's lives and well-being are at stake and huge amounts of money are being allocated to deal with societal conditions.

Fortunately, social scientists have developed ways of making observation systematic so that the number of plausible alternative explanations for the impact of any program can be reduced. These methods grew out of the attempt of scientists from all fields to conduct experiments so that the effect of particular factors could be isolated to estimate their importance. Unfortunately, those evaluating social programs cannot use many of the approaches developed by laboratory scientists (e.g., chemists) for many reasons that will become apparent as you proceed through this chapter. However, two classes of design--pre-experimental and quasi-experiment can frequently be used. They will be presented after the discussion of some basic terms.

PART 2: BASIC CONCEPTS NECESSARY TO UNDERSTAND TYPES OF RESEARCH DESIGNS

Regardless of design, all attempts at evaluating the impact of a social program consider at least the following nine basic concepts discussed below.

You may be familiar with some or all of these concepts. For that reason, you should read only those sections of this part unfamiliar to you.

The material in this part is presented in a glossary format. The concepts are applied throughout the remainder of this chapter. The purpose here is merely to make sure that you have a general comprehension of what they mean.

Definitions

1. Dependent Variable

The dependent variable is the condition which the researcher is interested in explaining. It may be the math ability of high school students, the fluctuations in the oil market, or the effects of compensatory education on preschoolers. In the pill-taking example the dependent variable is the change in your health status. In all cases, the aim is to explain why a variable behaves the way it does.

2. Independent Variable

The independent variable is the variable used to explain the one that is dependent. It is usually thought of as being casually prior to the dependent variable. In the study of compensatory education the independent variable could be the type of education presented to the preschoolers. In the pill-taking example the independent variable is the pill.

3. Manipulation

Manipulation occurs when an experimenter can intentionally create variations in the independent variable. These manipulations could be different approaches to teaching preschoolers or the race of the teacher. In the pill-taking example one manipulation could be the strength of the dosage used in the pill. Another manipulation could be the type of drug used.

4. Confounding Variable

Confounding variables are the rival explanations for the behavior of the dependent variable. The difference in the amount of learning by preschoolers may not be due to different approaches to teaching but to factors outside the classroom such as home environment, or the number of siblings. In the pill-taking example the improvement in health may be due to changes in eating habits, more sleep, or any of a host of alternative explanations.

5. Subjects

Subjects are the units upon which the observations are made. They may include the individual preschoolers, nation-states, formal organizations, or government agencies. In the pill-taking example you are the subject upon which the observation is made.

6. Control

There is within every evaluation either explicit or implicit comparison: that some collection of subjects is better or worse as a result of the evaluator's treatment or manipulation. The control is that set of data with which the treatment group is compared. The control can be another collection of subjects not receiving the treatment or it can be a series of measurements taken on the treatment group before it receives the treatment.

7. Randomization

Randomization is the process by which subjects have an equal chance of being assigned to either the treatment group or the control group. The group they end up in is determined purely by chance.

The last two items (8 and 9) pertain to "validity," a term that has numerous meanings. Some consider the term to mean "truthfulness" while others consider it to mean "usefulness." Some distinguish between the reliability of results (can the experiment be repeated), while others consider reliability to be a question of the validity of the study. The definitions provided below distinguish between internal and external validity. They will be defined briefly and used throughout the chapter in the way in which they are defined here.

8. Internal Validity

This term asks the question "did the experiment cause the results that the program evaluator reported?" It is a question that relates to many of the considerations raised in the first part of this chapter. In assessing the impact of the medicine, we discovered that there were many rival explanations. The extent to which a study has internal validity is the extent to which it determines that the program rather than some other factor "caused" the impact on society.

9. External Validity

This term asks the question "to what population and settings can this effect be generalized?" Assuming that a study has internal validity and demonstrates that a given social program resulted in a given social effect, it must still be determined whether this effect could be expected under similar conditions in other settings. External validity is important because it provides decision-makers with a basis for determining whether a given social program should be applied somewhere else.

PART 3: DESIGNS

The presentation of designs which follow will use the code and graphic presentation developed by Campbell and Stanley. An X will refer to the exposure of a group to an experimental treatment or event, the effects of which are to be measured in some fashion. An O represents a process of observation or measurement. The X's and O's in a given row are applied to the same people or groups. The left-to-right dimension symbolizes the temporal order in which events occur. The X's and O's on top of each other are simultaneous occurrences. The symbol R stands for the random assignment of subjects to separate treatment groups. This randomization occurs at a specific time and is general procedure used to bring about pretreatment equality of groups. The graphic presentation of parallel rows not separated by dashes represents comparison groups equated by randomization, while those separated by a dashed line are comparison groups not equated due to lack of random assignment. Six different designs ranging in general from weakest to strongest will be presented below.

One-Shot Case Study

In this design, a single group is studied only once after being exposed to some treatment which is presumed to cause a change in the dependent variable. The diagram of such a study is:

$$X \qquad O$$

These studies have such a total lack of control as to be almost no value to the evaluator. Fortunately, this kind of design is almost never used in serious program evaluation. The design is discussed mainly as a minimum starting point. Underlying all program evaluation is the process of comparison, of noting differences or of contrasting the changes in the dependent variable. For such comparisons to be some value, the things being compared should be observed with equal care. In this design, a thoroughly studied single case is implicitly compared to what would have been had the X not occurred. Studies using this design often collect copious amount of data on the treatment group in order to buttress their conclusions. However, these types of studies suffer from what Campbell and Stanley call the error of "misplaced precision" since this potentially vast amount of data in no way compensates for lack of an explicit comparison with some other group or set of observations. The One-Shot Case Study is the weakest design to be considered here and is even less complex than the pill-taking exercise discussed below.

One Group Pretest/Posttest

This is the design used in the pill-taking exercise. In general, the design looks like this:

$$O_1 \qquad\qquad X \qquad\qquad O_2$$

At O_1, the pretest, you observe that you are not feeling well. You go to the Health Center for the pill treatment, X. One day later at O_2, the posttest, you notice an improvement in your health status. The discussion of this design and the ones that follow will make a small change in the pill-taking example. Assume that from now on you are part of a larger group of people given the same drug. This change is done because all serious program evaluation are based on studying large numbers of cases, not a single individual. The pill-taking example will be used to illustrate the strengths and weaknesses of this design.

There are several confounding variables which threaten this design. These confounding variables offer rival explanations to the hypothesis that X was responsible for the difference between O_1 and O_2.

The first of these uncontrolled confounding variables is history. Between the pretest observation and the posttest observations, many other change-inducing events could have taken place besides the experimental treatment. After a winter of drab and depressing days the sun might have come bursting out with all its warmth on the day that you went down to the Health Center. Thus, the reason you feel better may be due to the beautiful day rather than the pill you took. In order to be a reasonable rival hypothesis, the event should have occurred to most of the people in the group. History becomes a more credible rival hypothesis for explaining the change, the longer the lapse between the pretest/posttest.

A second rival explanation is maturation. These are all the organic or institutional processes that systematically change with the passage of time, irrespective of particular external events.

While this is not a likely explanation for the change that occurred in your health status, due to the short period of time between O_1 and O_2, it does become a more plausible rival hypothesis as the time between O_1 and O_2 increases,

A third possible explanation is the effect of testing -- the effect of O_1 itself. While this would be a doubtful explanation in the pill-taking example, it is known that subjects taking an achievement test for the second time, O_2, usually do better than those taking the test for the first time, O_1.

As the problem of testing exemplifies, the program evaluator has to be sensitive to the reactivity of the instruments used to measure change in the dependent variable. In any scientific experiment or field application of a treatment, the process of measuring may change that which is being observed. We can expect this reactivity to be a factor in all cases except those where the measuring process is a passive recorder of behavior. An example of a passive measuring process is using the amount of finger-prints on the glass in front of a museum exhibit as an indicator of the popularity of that exhibit. In the pill-taking example, this problem is a possibility if some members of the group want to impress the doctor when he asks, "how are you feeling?"

A fourth possible problem is instrumentation. This refers to changes in the measuring instrument, which might explain the difference between the pretest and posttest. For instance, human observers might become more skillful as they become more familiar with the testing procedure. On the other hand, the pill-taking example, the difference between O_1 and O_2, for some members of the group might be explained by the doctor becoming more fatigued as the day passes, which in turn influences his judgement.

A fifth rival hypothesis is statistical regression. If subjects were chosen because of their extreme scores on some testing instruments at time O_1, then one would expect a number of them to regress to the mean naturally. This regression would thus confound the experimental results. In the pill-taking example, this is a distinct possibility since you were chosen because of your poor health--an extreme score. One would expect a certain number of subjects in your group to regress to the mean, i.e., to improve their health status, regardless of the treatment given.

While this design is still a weak one, it is enough of an improvement over the One-Shot Case Study to be used when none of the other designs described below are possible.

Static-Group Comparison

Suppose the Health Center compared the results of your treatment group with another group of students. Such an evaluation design is called a Static-Group Comparison. In this design, a group which was exposed to treatment X is compared to one which was not. This comparison is made to establish the effect of X.

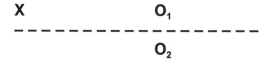

The hope is that the two groups will be equal and thus a valid comparison can be made. Unfortunately, there is no formal way of confirming that the groups would have been equivalent had it not been for the treatment X. This problem, indicated by the dotted line, highlights the major confounding variable not controlled by this design—selection. If O_1 and O_2 differ, this occurrence might well have happened because different criteria were used to place people in one group or the other. Thus, the groups would have differed even without the experimental treatment. Selection could be a problem in the pill-taking example if the Health Center put all the sick people in one group and at the time of observation O_2, selected an equal number of healthy students as the comparison group. Since one would not expect all the sick people to be completely cured, the Health Center might falsely conclude that the drug did not have an effect. In fact, this would not be the case since there is no reason to assume that the two groups were equal had it not been for the taking of the pill.

Another confounding variable associated with this design is experimental mortality. Mortality produces O_1-O_2 changes due to the differential drop-out rates of subjects between the two groups. In the pill-taking example, some students who improved their health status might not feel the need to return to the Health Center to report their change in health status, thus distorting the composition of the treatment group.

Time-Series

Since the withholding of treatment is morally wrong, the Health Center might want to turn to a Quasi-Experimental Design to evaluate the efficacy of the drug. Suppose that it measured the individual health status of a group of students over an extended period of time. During that time students periodically reported to the Health Center for an examination. At some point in this series of examinations, the Health Center gave the drug to the students. The design would look like the following:

$$O_1 O_2 O_3 O_4 X O_5 O_6 O_7 O_8$$

Basically, the Time-Series Design contains a series of observations or measurements on a group or individual and the presentation of a treatment manipulation into this time series. The results of treatment are indicated by a discontinuity in the observations made during the time series.

Figure 1 represents some of the likely results for a time-series design into which a treatment, X, has been presented to the subjects. It appears from Figure 1 that the treatment had some impact in the case of A and B and conceivably, in the case of C, D, and E. It would not appear that the treatment had any impact in the case of F, G, and H.

**TREATMENT
X**

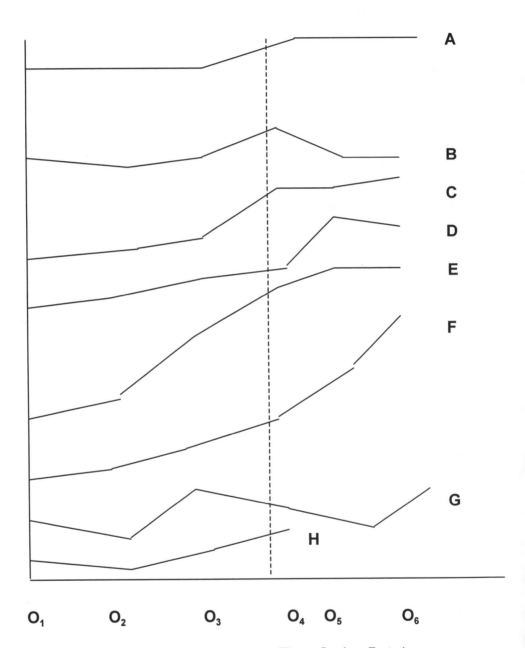

Figure 1: Potential Impact of Treatment on Time-Series Data*

* adapted from Campbell and Stanley (1963).

The most obvious weakness of this design is the threat posed by history. There may be some event external to the treatment session that caused the change in the dependent variable. To the degree that you can reasonably discount such outside events as causing the change in the dependent variable, you increase the strength of the inferences made from the experimental results. As was noted in the One-Group Pretest/Posttest, this design is susceptible to the confounding influences of a sunny day, which might occur at the same time the Health Center gave you the pill.

While this design will never prove the efficacy of a treatment as a true experimental design can, it should be used where nothing better can be carried out. Although this design is not definitive the results of any one study are strengthened if they can be replicated in different settings.

Nonequivalent Control Group

This is one of the most popular quasi-experimental designs for program evaluation. Suppose that the Health Center wished to use two different dormitories as subject pools for its study concerning the effectiveness of the drug. All the students are given a pretest examination and later a posttest. In between tests the experimental group is given the pill. The design would look like the following:

$$O_1 \qquad X \qquad O_2$$
$$\text{-----------------------}$$
$$O_3 \qquad\qquad O_4$$

In general, this design consists of an experimental and control group whose equivalence has not been assured by the random assignment of subjects to the groups. As much as possible, the evaluator tries to find groups that are as similar as possible.

It is assumed that the evaluator has control over which group is presented with the treatment and that assignment is random. This design should not be confused with the Pretest/Posttest Control Group Design. In the present design, the subjects are *not* randomly assigned to groups from a common population. The more comparable the experimental and the control group are in terms of recruitment and scores on the pretest, the more powerful this design becomes.

The more equal the two groups are the more one can expect this design to control for the main effects of history, maturation, testing, and instrumentation. As in the Pretest/Posttest Control Group Design, history maturation, testing, and instrumentation should not be threats to internal validity since they will affect both groups equally. However, you should be aware that intrasession history could be a threat to internal validity. Assuming that the two dormitories were roughly equal, then this design will control for such effects as a sunny day or the doctor's fatigue.

Even with the problems associated with this design, the addition of a nonequivalent control group makes it much stronger than the One-Group Pretest/Posttest Design.

Multiple Time-Series

Suppose that, in addition to the time-series data collected for the previous design, the Health Center corresponded with another university health center and asked it to collect a similar time series without the treatment, X, being presented. The basic design could be diagrammed as follows:

$$O_1 O_2 O_3 O_4 X O_5 O_6 O_7 O_8$$
$$\overline{\hspace{4cm}}$$
$$O_9 O_{10} O_{11} O_{12} O_{13} O_{14} O_{15} O_{16}$$

In essence, this design is a combination of the Nonequivalent Control Group Design and the Time-Series Design. In most evaluations of this type, evaluators obtain their data from a similar institution which is not exposed to the treatment.

The design contains within it the strengths of the two previous quasi-experimental designs. In addition, any change in the dependent variable cased by the treatment is confirmed twice, first against the control group and second against its own pre-X observations.

This design controls for the possibility of selection-maturation interaction being a rival hypothesis. For that interaction to be true, the treatment group would have to show a greater rate of gain, which would be noticeable in the pre-x observations.

The threat of history as a rival hypothesis remains valid in this design. The improvement in your group's health status could be due to the fact that it was sunny and bright at your university, while the control group was having a drab and rainy day.

As with the Time-Series Design, this design is susceptible to the threat of external validity coming from a testing-X interaction. One solution to this problem is to use non-reactive tests wherever possible.

The Multiple Time-Series Design is the best and most highly recommended of the designs presented here. However, it may not be possible to use a Multiple Time Series in many studies. In those cases, other designs should be used. In any case, when trying to assess if a policy works, always think about plausible alternative explanations and how to eliminate them.

Chapter 18

How the PRINCE System Produced the American Constitution

*This chapter is taken from *Everyman's Prince* written by William D. Coplin and Michael L. O'Leary in 1976. In this chapter the term salience is used in the place of priority in the Prince analysis.

YOUR GOAL

To understand how the prince system can be used to describe the outcome of the constitutional convention.

One of the mysteries of the American Constitutional Convention is **why** George Washington remained so passive during its sessions yet emerged from the convention as the first American political superstar. It can now be revealed that Washington was not passive at all, but was very actively, if quietly, applying a PRINCE analysis to what was happening. Many people then—and now—have thought that Washington was just another pretty face without any political skills to match his military successes. It has been argued that in politics he was just a front man for clever Machiavellian politicians. The truth of the matter is that he was himself a skillful politician employing the appropriate PRINCE charts at every occasion. Washington earned the title "father of his country," by first becoming every American's Prince.

In fewer than four months about forty men wrote a document that was a masterpiece and resolved the differences of a diverse collection of anti-British rebels who had only just begun to develop a conception of an American nation. Such a document was not produced before 1787, nor has one been produced since. At least one good explanation for what is universally ranked as one of the wonders of the political world is that someone was working the PRINCE accounting system. It seems clear to us that it had to be Washington, with his experience as a surveyor and his familiarity with using charts to get the lay of the land. While the rest of the guys were boozing it up in the Indian Queen, a local pub, on the evening of May 27, 1787, Washington was busy in his room with four empty PRINCE accounting system charts.

His first job was to reduce the forty-odd delegates to a manageable number of political actors. His limit, as we indicated in the first chapter, was ten political actors.

He was helped in this task first by the rules of the convention that provided for voting by state delegations rather than individuals. He had to deal with only twelve actors—the thirteen former colonies minus Rhode Island, whose delegates boycotted the meeting. This was probably close enough to the ideal upper limit of ten, but because it was summer Washington looked for other ways to make his job easier by reducing the number of actors.

> PRINCiple 3.1:* To simplify the PRINCE charts, lump
> together actors who have strong common interests.

For the sake of simplicity, George Washington lumped the actors together. Washington called South Carolina, North Carolina, and Georgia the *Deep South*. The Deep South states had similar economic interests that were different from those of the North, including most significantly a reliance upon slave labor. Therefore Washington expected, quite rightly, that they would act together on a wide range of issues. George called New Jersey, Delaware, Connecticut, New York, and Maryland the *States' Righters*. The States' Righters were small states worried about their continued influence in any new arrangements, plus New York, a majority of whose delegates also worried about states' rights because they wanted a weak central government. George treated Massachusetts and New Hampshire as one. These two states also had similar economic interests, plus a long background of cultural affinity and close cooperation between their citizens. There were only two states treated separately—Pennsylvania, the state of Ben Franklin, and George's own state, Virginia. Washington thus ended up with five actors: (1) the Deep South, (2) the States' Righters, (3) Massachusetts-New Hampshire, (4) Pennsylvania, and (5) Virginia.

After defining the actors, George got out his PRINCE charts and went to the next problem—identifying issues. The first issue was whether the convention would try to make the thirteen states into one nation or just strengthen their existing alliance against England. The convention had been organized for the official purpose of amending the old constitution, the Articles of Confederation. But Washington and some of the other leaders, like Benjamin Franklin, thought that the old constitution was such a mess that an entirely new one should be written.

*Look for these inserts throughout the case studies in each section. They summarize important points made by the case.

Although there was a consensus that there should be a supreme court in the capital, not all agreed that there should be federal courts in the states. Hence, Issue 8 was whether the federal courts should operate within states.

Realizing that the delegates would probably spend most of the beautiful summer of 1787 cooped up indoors debating these eight substantive issues, George knew that they would still have two very important procedural issues left: (1) how the Constitution was to be amended and (2) how the Constitution was to be ratified. Having gotten wind of the scuttlebut from the delegates, Washington knew that amending the Constitution would be Issue 9—whether the delegates would accept a proposed amendment procedure that allowed the Constitution to be amended by three-fourths of the states or would favor some other plan such as unanimous consent by all the states, which would in effect give each state a veto.

Washington's final issue dealt with the ratification process. He defined Issue 10 as the ratification of the Constitution by the people rather than by the states through their legislatures.

Washington could have defined a number of other issues, but he felt that these gave him enough of an idea of the major disputes and results of the convention. He then made a list of the ten issues and a label for each issue that he would use on his PRINCE charts. The list was:

1. The purpose of the convention is to write a new constitution and thereby create a nation. Label: *Nation*.
2. A strong executive will be created. Label: *Exec*.
3. People shall elect the president. Label: *Presid*.
4. Representation in the legislature will be according to population. Label: *Legis*.
5. Slaves will be counted as part of a state's population. Label: *Slaves*.
6. Congress will have the power to tax exports. Label: *Exports*.
7. Congress will have the power to regulate, and hence to abolish, the slave trade. Label: *Slave Trade*.
8. Federal courts shall be established in the states. Label: *Courts*.
9. Only three-fourths of the states are needed to amend the Constitution. Label: *Amend*.
10. Ratification of the Constitution by the people. Label: *Ratif*.

Having identified the basic issues as well as the primary political actors, Washington now had the columns and rows of the four PRINCE

CHART 3-1. Political actors' issue positions.

Actors	Issues				
	Nation	Exec.	Presid.	Legis.	Slaves
Deep South					
(Ga., S.C., N.C.)	+3	+3	+2	+3	+3
States' Righters					
(N.Y., N.J., Del., Conn., Md.)	-3	-1	-3	-3	-2
Massachusetts-New Hampshire	+3	+3	+3	0	-3
Pennsylvania	+3	+3	+3	-3	-3
Virginia	+3	0	+3	+3	+3
	Exports	Slave trade	Courts	Amend.	Ratif.
Deep South					
(Ga., S.C., N.C.)	-3	-3	-3	-3	+3
States' Righters					
(N.Y., N.J., Del., Conn., Md.)	+2	+2	-2	-2	+1
Massachusetts-New Hampshire	0	+2	+3	+3	+3
Pennsylvania	+2	+2	+3	+2	+3
Virginia	-3	+2	+3	+2	+2

charts labeled. He then proceeded to estimate the numbers necessary to fill up the cells of the charts.

> PRINCiple 3.3: Use the PRINCE system to project the voting decisions of legislative bodies.

He started with the issue position—Chart 3-1. He scored a +3 when there was agreement among the members of the coalitions for a particular formulation and -3 when there was agreement against it. When there was not full agreement, he scored somewhere between 1 and 3, depending upon how strong a consensus was for or against the proposal among each coalition-actor.

Washington then moved on to Chart 3-2—the power of each actor for each issue. He gave each group a power of 1, except the States' Righters, whom he gave a power of 2. He thus employed an abbreviated form of Chart 3-2.

The information in Chart 3-3 proved critical for Washington and the American Constitutional Convention because it registered the salience of the issues for each of the actors. Chart 3-3 indicates the importance Washington thought each of the actors had for each of the issues. One can see how critical salience is by first multiplying Charts 3-1 and

CHART 3-2. Power of the actors on issues.

Actors	Power for all issues
Deep South (Ga., S.C., N.C.)	1
States' Righters (N.Y., N.J., Del., Conn., Md.)	2
Massachusetts-New Hampshire	1
Pennsylvania	1
Virginia	1

3-2 and comparing the product to Charts 3-1, 3-2, and 3-3 multiplied together. Chart 3-4 presents the sums of the columns, which is an indicator of what is likely to happen.

If salience were not figured into the PRINCE system, Washington would have been particularly despondent. Without salience, there seems to be only clearcut support for the ratification procedure and a strong executive. All the rest of the figures are borderline. However, the addition of salience indicates a strong commitment for creating a union, a strong executive, counting slaves as population, and the amendment and ratification procedures. There also appears to be a strong commitment against a legislature based on a proportion of the population and the power of Congress to tax exports.

> PRINCiple 3.4:   Always remember to consider salience when making a compromise. It's frequently prudent to offer a little extra to the side with the higher salience.

Washington assumed that 20 points was a cutoff for consensus on an issue (+ for and - against) and concluded that a large number of compromises would be necessary to produce a strong constitution. Realizing the need for compromise, he formulated a strategy on his part that would keep any single political actor from pulling out of the convention. To help him do this, he completed Chart 3-5 of the PRINCE system.

Washington was particularly wary of *polarization*, a phenomenon that has rendered many meetings and some political systems hopelessly confused. Polarization is the degree to which the political actors are split into two opposing camps. The degree to which there are no actors in the system who are friendly with the enemies of other actors is an

CHART 3-3. Salience of actors on issues.

Actors	Issues				
	Nation	Exec.	Presid.	Legis.	Slaves
Deep South					
(Ga., S.C., N.C.)	3	2	1	2	3
States' Righters					
(N.Y., N.J., Del., Conn., Md.)	2	3	2	3	1
Massachusetts-New Hampshire	3	2	1	3	1
Pennsylvania	3	2	1	3	1
Virginia	3	3	1	3	3
	Exports	Slave trade	Courts	Amend.	Ratif.
Deep South					
(Ga., S.C., N.C.)	3	3	3	1	1
States' Righters					
(N.Y., N.J., Del., Conn., Md.)	3	1	2	1	1
Massachusetts-New Hampshire	3	1	2	3	1
Pennsylvania	2	1	3	3	1
Virginia	3	0	3	3	2

indication of polarization. In contrast, the degree to which friends and enemies are thoroughly mixed indicates a basically depolarized system.

> PRINCiple 3.5: Polarization is destructive and consensus is constructive if you are on the side of the consensus. If you are not, the converse is true.

Washington employed a simple procedure for calculating the polarization level of the convention. He ranked all pairs of actors at the convention as friendly, neutral, or hostile. Chart 3-6 indicates how the political actors were ordered.

Washington breathed a sigh of relief when he examined the list. He discovered that the actors were relatively depolarized, because Virginia as well as Massachusetts-New Hampshire provided friendly links between most of the hostile pairs. The major threat of polarization came from the fact that the States' Righters group was hostile toward both Pennsylvania and Virginia and the Deep South was also hostile towards Pennsylvania. This situation created the possibility of two camps forming—one around Pennsylvania and Virginia and the other around the Deep South and States' Righters. Although the situation was relatively depolarized at the outset, conditions existed for hostility be-

CHART 3-4. Predicted issue outcomes with and without salience.

	Issues				
	Nation	*Exec.*	*Presid.*	*Legis.*	*Slaves*
Charts 3-1 × 3-2 *(Without Salience)*	+6	+7	+5	-3	-4
Charts 3-1 × 3-2 × 3-3 *(With Salience)*	+24	+12	+5	-12	+8
	Exports	*Slave trade*	*Courts*	*Amend.*	*Ratif.*
Charts 3-1 × 3-2 *(Without Salience)*	0	+7	+2	0	+13
Charts 3-1 × 3-2 × 3-3 *(With Salience)*	-2	-1	+7	+14	+15

CHART 3-5. Friendship-neutrality-hostility chart.

	Feels about this actor:				
This actor	*Deep South*	*States' Righters*	*Massachusetts-New Hampshire*	*Pennsylvania*	*Virginia*
Deep South		-	-	-	+
States' Righters	-		+	-	-
Massachusetts-New Hampshire	-	+		+	-
Pennsylvania	-	-	+		+
Virginia	+	-	-	+	

tween the two potential camps to grow and for the convention to fail as a result of that growth.

Fortunately, Washington had a couple of things going for him. One of the most important was that he was a member of the prestigious Virginia delegation. Realizing that he was something of a national hero, he concluded that if he took public positions and got involved directly in the issues, he would generate a break between the camps. He concluded that his role was to be passive in public and at formal meetings but to work actively for compromise behind the scenes. He could also keep Virginia from antagonizing the States' Righters if he played a consensus-building role.

Washington also was fortunate to have Benjamin Franklin in the Pennsylvania delegation. By far, Benjamin was *the* star of the con-

CHART 3-6. Pairs of actors ordered from friendly to neutral to hostile.

Pair of actors	Friendship-neutrality-hostility score
Pennsylvania-Virginia	+
Pennsylvania-Massachusetts/New Hampshire	+
Deep South-Virginia	+
States' Righters-Massachusetts/New Hampshire	+
Deep South-Massachusetts/New Hampshire	−
Virginia-Massachusetts/New Hampshire	−
Deep South-States' Righters	−
Deep South-Pennsylvania	−
Pennsylvania-States' Righters	−
Virginia-States' Righters	−

vention which meant that Pennsylvania delegates would follow his lead and that delegations from other states would be open to his views. Washington got to him before the convention and convinced him (we are not sure whether he used the PRINCE system or just appealed to Franklin's enormous ego) to modify Pennsylvania's view and to seek compromise with the other states.

Another fortunate factor that operated to the advantage of those who wanted a successful convention was that the States' Righters and the Deep South had a moderate degree of antagonism toward each other. Washington's plan—to make sure that the two groups did not form a coalition against the rest of the actors—was greatly aided by the basic antagonism the two groups had for each other. It was not a sufficiently strong antagonism to prevent them from cooperating (as was, for example, the antagonism between Virginia and the States' Righters) but it was sufficient to prevent the two groups from joining together and wrecking the convention.

PRINCiple 3.6: Compromise occurs on issues about which there is no consensus if actors have a consensus on other issues.

The charts helped Washington in many ways. For example, he could see that the strong executive (Issue 2) was uncertain of victory. The favorable actors—Deep South, Massachusetts-New Hampshire, and Pennsylvania—had only six votes (out of twelve). Washington's own state,

197

CHART 3-7. Score sheet comparing the PRINCE system to actual results.

	PRINCE analysis of events most likely to occur	
Issue	PRINCE total score	Actual results
1 (Nation)	+24	Occurred as stated
10 (Ratif.)	+15	Occurred as stated
9 (Amend.)	+14	Occurred as stated
2 (Exec.)	+12	Occurred as stated
5 (Slaves)	+8	Occurred but with slaves counting as three-fifths
8 (Courts)	+7	Compromise by leaving to Congress to decide
3 (Presid.)	+5	Compromise using electoral college instead of people
7 (Slave Trade)	−1	No regulating until 1808
6 (Exports)	−2	Rejected as stated
4 (Legis.)	−12	Most highly debated issue with a 50-50 compromise effected

Virginia, was so evenly divided that the delegation frequently was deadlocked and was unable to vote. (Note that Virginia has a zero issue position, but a saliency of 3 on this issue.) The idea was to get some of the States' Righters, who were only moderately opposed, to support a strong executive. As he looked at his friendship-neutrality-hostility chart he could see that it would be very unwise for anyone from Pennsylvania or the Deep South to lobby for a strong executive. The States' Righters had hostility toward both Pennsylvania and the Deep South. However, the Massachusetts-New Hampshire group was viewed more positively by the States' Righters, so Washington knew that they would be more likely to listen favorably to appeals from one of the New England delegation.

Washington also used his PRINCE calculations to plan where and how to make compromises that led to a successful consensus. On the question whether to count slaves as part of the population, it was clear that some compromise would have to be made. At first Washington thought of proposing to split the difference and count slaves as one-half, which is a common bargaining strategy. But he looked at the salience figures and saw that the proponents of counting slaves, the Deep South and Virginia, held their view with higher salience than the opponents who did not want to count slaves at all. So he suggested giving the South and Virginia slightly more than half and counting slaves as three-fifths of the population—bizarre from a humanistic viewpoint, but quite sound politically. On the other hand, when Washington looked at the salience for how legislative representation should be based (Issue 4) he saw that both sides held their views with equally high salience. Therefore he was attracted to the notion—which was finally accepted—of having two houses of the legislature, one to satisfy the views of each side.

It should also be clear that the decisions made by the convention rarely placed the States' Righters and the Deep South on the same side. A decision not to count slaves but to use proportional representation for determining representatives to the legislature would have done this. Instead, there was a compromise on both issues so that neither side would be alienated.

Another strategy followed by the convention was to avoid certain critical issues. Hence, the decision to end the importation of slaves was not to take effect until 1808—twenty-one years after the convention—and the question of the role of the federal courts was to be dealt with in the Congress itself.

Two of the time-worn patterns of compromise appeared to be most important here: One is to give each party half of the pie, which was implemented in the decisions on proportional representation and counting slaves, and the other is to postpone the consequence of the decision, if not the decision itself.

The PRINCE system gave Washington a picture of the areas of conflict and the actors most likely to disagree. As Table 3-7 shows, it forecast the convention results with notable accuracy. From this picture he was able to create an atmosphere of compromise by playing a quiet and unifying public role and a private role that worked for compromise. Fortunately for him and the new union, the predispositions of the actors were basically in the direction with which Washington agreed, which allowed him to play a consensus role in dealing with the convention. As we will see in the next chapter, it is sometimes necessary for those using the PRINCE system to play the role of breaking up existing agreements to get basic change. During the Constitutional Convention, Washington had only to insure an atmosphere of trust and compromise to achieve his purposes.